Beware the Financial-Industrial Complex

Strategies for Investing in a Corporatist World

Beware the Financial-Industrial Complex

Strategies for Investing in a Corporatist World

David G. Shink, CFP®

3/25/10

JB,
I am the lucky
person in my friendship
with you.

D S

iUniverse, Inc.
New York Bloomington

Beware The Financial Industrial Complex
Strategies for Investing in a Corporatist World

iUniverse books may be ordered through booksellers or by contacting:

iUniverse
1663 Liberty Drive
Bloomington, IN 47403
www.iuniverse.com
1-800-Authors (1-800-288-4677)

Because of the dynamic nature of the Internet, any Web addresses or links contained in this book may have changed since publication and may no longer be valid. The views expressed in this work are solely those of the author and do not necessarily reflect the views of the publisher, and the publisher hereby disclaims any responsibility for them.

ISBN: 9-781-4401-1446-5 (pbk)
ISBN: 9-781-4401-1447-2 (ebk)

Printed in the United States of America

iUniverse rev. date: 1/2/2009

For my Girls

Rhonda, Kyra, Hannah, and Trisch

Of Course my Bro – Kevan

Most of all for Ronald S. Shink, father, mentor and best friend.

Acknowledgments

My father, Ronald S. Shink, was a vigorous seeker of financial and business knowledge. I grew up in a home that was filled with ever-growing quantities of books, magazines, and newspapers. The notion of reading to understand the answers to money and wealth questions was a way of life for my father.

As a youth, I was not all that interested in seeking knowledge, investment or otherwise. Baseball was my first love. I remember my dad, when hearing of my desire to become a baseball player, sat me down, compelled to break down the mathematical impossibility of my achieving that dream. He also stressed that, at 10 years of age, pro potential would already be evident. If I wasn't already the best kid, not just on my team, but in the city, I had virtually no chance of turning pro. He advised me to pick a more realistic goal.

It took me a while to come into alignment with this realist philosophy. When I reached the age of 14, I landed my first job at a Greek restaurant. My dad decided that some of my earnings should be placed in the stock of a fast-growing local company called Kmart. I was not too fond of his idea. My plans were much more geared toward the day-to-day expenses of a teenage boy—rock-and-roll concert tickets, motorcycles, and the Holy Grail—my own car.

It was not until my early twenties, as I began to think about life after college, that my dad's outlook began to intrigue me. The late 1980s were interesting times for the markets. I remember October 19, 1987, vividly. While most of the students on campus seemed unconcerned, I was anxious. I knew my dad had a lot of investments and I was concerned for him, my family, and what impact the "crash" would have. I remember driving home and finding my dad in front of the TV watching a cable channel called Financial News Network. It was all very scary but somehow exciting. Dad said he didn't think that everything was worth 20 percent less than it was the day before and that, even if it were, it would not be a good time to sell.

We joked together that we could jump off a ledge, but our home in suburban Detroit had only two floors and there was no actual ledge to stand on. Humor was an important part of my dad's outlook. Laughter seemed to bring great comfort to him and, when he was on a mission to make you laugh, you had better be sure not to have any food or drink in your mouth.

He would tell me long stories about his business dealings, going deep into the minutia of the people involved and his decision processes. Looking at business and the people he knew was endlessly interesting to Dad. He was an avid student of the grand business stories, and he devoured books on business failures, scams, and other interesting nonfiction material.

Our discussions were most often analytical, about politics and business. He and I spent hours on the lead-up to the US invasion of Iraq in March 2003. It saddened him to watch the suffering and, particularly, the US casualties. He was a man of great emotion and sensitivity, although those who did not see these moments remember him as a bit coarse and outspoken.

I look back on those days and see them as a wonderful stroke of luck: I was raised and spent many of my adult years with a very insightful mentor. He was quite a unique person and my father, to boot. I realize more every day that I am lucky to have had my dad as my best friend. I miss my father more the longer he is gone. If it were not for his strong personality and influence on me, I would not have the foundation that allows me to see the world from his unique Shink perspective.

I also remember my good fortune to speak at my father's funeral with great fondness for my best friend, mentor, provider, and dad. It is a rare moment in life, or sadly in mourning, to be able to speak from your heart with true love and feeling. The key thing that I voiced was that my dad did not see the glass as half empty or half full, but, rather, he saw the glass. He tried to see the world as it was, and to create a life strategy from there. He was not an optimist or a pessimist, but a staunch realist. Continuously striving to understand the world the way it is, with as much objectivity and realism as possible, is to live life while seeing the glass—the world as it really is.

My mother, Patricia Shink, was also a driving influence on my outlook toward life. In contrast to my dad's pragmatic realism, I was lucky enough to have a mother with deep sensitivity and insight. Her caring and nurturing allowed me to develop a respect for myself and others in many important ways.

Mom was always there to support me and to help work through the stress and challenge of becoming a brother, a man, and a father. She is a person who has faced many challenges without ever backing down. I hope that one day I will begin to live up to the incredible standard she set by her example. As indelible as my father's mark upon my being, it could never have been absorbed without the nurturing and care of Mom. She gave me the strength and character that have carried me through my lowest and most difficult moments, without which I would be much less of a man today.

My good fortune to have been raised by two very high-quality individuals has also been enhanced by my brother Kevan. Kevan has faced difficult challenges as an individual with mild cerebral palsy along with developmental disabilities. Kevan has many of the things we all take for granted unavailable to him—things like driving a car and making day-to-day decisions are not options for him. The challenges that Kevan faces have brought me perspective and gratitude for my ability to simply function on a daily basis. Developing understanding and sensitivity for individuals with developmental disabilities is something toward which I continually strive. All of us are only one accident or misstep away from having to rely on others for our welfare, financial management, and other daily affairs.

Finally, my wife Rhonda has been a huge pillar of strength as I have built my professional and personal life. Without her unyielding confidence and encouragement, I would not be nearly the father or husband I am today. I cannot overstate her contribution to everything that I am as a man and that we are as a family.

As I have built my professional practice as an advisor, I have faced challenges and gone down many blind alleys. Without Rhonda's patience and care, her strength, and her awesome cooking, I would have a much lower quality of life. Together, Rhonda and I are traveling a path of incredible beauty in our relationship and in the raising of our two daughters, Kyra and Hannah.

My daughters are the greatest gift of all. They continuously give me love, strength, and the greatest reason to live life to the highest level that is possible for me. Kyra and Hannah are the gift of life that Rhonda and I have been blessed with in the way only a parent can understand. Fulfilling my role as a parent is an extreme challenge that I learn from each and every day. I could not have been more fortunate to have such a wonderful family to love and have to love me.

Introduction

I began investing in 1978 at the age of 14. It would be many years before I began to develop a philosophical framework within which to think about money and investing. After completing my undergraduate studies at the University of Michigan in 1988, I worked daily with my father, who also happened to be my mentor, for my real education in business, investing, and responsible life choices.

When I entered the business of providing financial advice in 1992, I underwent an additional intensive phase of learning. Early in my professional career, I decided to acquire as many professional licenses as I could. I also decided to pursue the Certified Financial Planner® designation, which I completed in May 1995. I undertook these classes and exams because I wanted to be a credible, ethical, and sophisticated financial advisor. I wanted to be ready and able to answer any client questions and understand all types of financial situations.

Most of what I learned in my formal education dissipated quickly after the exams. I do treasure those pursuits, but I cannot say that I use more than a little of the formal knowledge that I gathered. I feel strongly that what was gained by my brain and psyche was an ability and aptitude to think through financial and personal dilemmas. Education helped me learn the process of problem solving, but rarely are investment decisions directly addressed in books.

There was also much to learn about financial regulation. Much of the material required in securities licensing revolves around market rules and consumer protection. As these rules grow ever more complex, I have become a cynic and outspoken critic of what I see as a financial system that is overwhelmingly incomprehensible to the majority of investors.

It is striking that the financial licensing and professional preparation process involves no Hippocratic oath. The creators, manufacturers, and marketers of financial products do not begin from the starting point of "first, do no harm." By its very nature, investing may do harm in ways that no one can predict due to market uncertainty and unpredictable future events. This future uncertainty can camouflage behavior that is counter to consumers' best interests. My assessment is that modern financial services firms have stayed extremely far away from the ideals of Hippocrates.

A significant period passed before I began to recognize my most important job as an advisor: communicating fundamental investment concepts, such as the difference between debt and equity investing. Helping those who came to me for advice to understand the basics of equity ownership and its challenges became my core mission. Investors came to me to find understanding and a resource that would first do no harm. They asked me questions, but not to obtain answers. The questions usually all led to the same goal … did I know the answer and, more importantly, could I be trusted?

As the years have passed, I have developed a growing belief that people are simply looking for competent guidance from a trustworthy source. They want to delegate their investment decisions to someone who will not abuse their trust.

My objective in this book is to break down the decisions we all face into the simple concepts that I have developed over my years of professional practice. I want to share my observations and concerns about the way consumers are treated in an incredibly complex financial world. Our financial life decisions do not need to be overwhelming. The core concern that I carry into every day and every decision is the fear that the financial industry machine is fraught with conflicts of interest.

I have a firm belief that complexity is almost never present in worthy financial concepts. Complexity, I believe, is a great predictor of poor financial results. I offer an initial list of important things to avoid:

- Complicated products

- Confusing or inconsistent explanations

- Future-looking predictions of complex processes (i.e., the economy, interest rates, market direction, political outcomes)

- Investment opportunities with unrealistic guaranteed rates of return

- Investments in the stock market without stock market risk

- Media hype of economic and market events

I viscerally dislike complexity. The core financial product that is the vehicle of choice for me is the tried and tested mutual fund. There will be no sophisticated forecasting techniques or financial secrets revealed in this book, just a collection of my philosophies for creating and maintaining financial strength through well-diversified portfolios of mutual funds with significant allocations of stocks.

Learning to escape the focus of market direction is a counter-intuitive notion. Every evening, the national news reports on the market direction for that day. We have all been taught to believe that the daily direction of the market has meaning. Big exciting media events are based on the Dow 10,000 or Dow 14,000 or a market day where the average moves 100, 200, or even 400 points. These can make for very entertaining news stories, but the sensational is likely to distract from attaining long-term growth and the creation of financial strength. Day to day, the market is a faddish, neurotic, bipolar being. These daily, quarterly, or even annual swings are a fact of life that will only become more intense and disturbing as our media and public psychology grow ever more intense.

Over the longer run of 3-, 5-, and 10-year time frames, the market is simply a place where pricing is negotiated. The long-term investor believes that ownership creates wealth and financial strength, and everything else is simply noise. This is the noise of those trying to predict the future of prices tomorrow, next week, or next quarter—an impossible feat. No one has or ever will predict the future with any consistent accuracy. This forms the central pillar of my investing philosophy—the wealth-creating process of owning quality equities over time. Simply put, it is the owners who will build wealth over time.

Daily market movements are crucial to traders, money managers, and others with hundreds of millions of dollars at their control. Minute to minute and tick to tick can mean everything. However, these short-term fluctuations have almost no meaning for the long-term investor. The media find excitement in the hot stocks and latest market moves. The current change in the value of the US dollar or the price of a barrel of oil is something that is reported constantly. Is this information of any use for long-term investors? No, not for the majority of us.

We need to understand, believe, and become loyal to the simple concept that ownership creates value, dividends, and growth over time. Ownership of quality companies is the answer to creating wealth. I put forth this simple truth: Quality ownership appreciates over time. Through the vehicle of mutual funds, an investor can own a diversified portfolio of quality US and global companies. Ownership in mutual funds provides professional management that creates monitoring and diversification, and helps investors avoid the day-to-day fluctuations that promote anxiety and cause you to think short term.

Contents

Corporatism

"I am convinced the prophets of doom have to be taken seriously."

Maurice Strong

Americans were warned in 1961 by President Dwight D. Eisenhower to beware the military-industrial complex: "The potential for the disastrous rise of misplaced power exists and will persist. We must never let the weight of this combination endanger our liberties or democratic processes. We should take nothing for granted. Only an alert and knowledgeable citizenry can compel the proper meshing of the huge industrial and military machinery of defense with our peaceful methods and goals so that security and liberty may prosper together."

This warning did not originate with President Eisenhower. Attempts to conceptualize something similar to a modern military-industrial complex existed before Eisenhower's address. In 1956, sociologist C. Wright Mills had claimed in his book, *The Power Elite*, that a cabal of business, political, and military leaders, motivated by mutual interests, constituted the real leaders of the state. Adherents to this theory would say that this political/economic system is effectively a dark force that is beyond democratic control.

As we enter the sixth year of the war in Iraq, we are again witnessing evidence of our failure to heed this warning. Whatever your political opinion, it is hard to deny that the US military has grown to shape the world in many ways. The law of unintended consequences prevails in much of the US military activity and its consequences post World War II. It is easy to develop a cynical view of what we are actually accomplishing in the massive expenditure of lives and wealth. These issues have grown so very complex that I often wonder who the "we" in Eisenhower's message is. Who is watching our liberties and protecting democracy? Can "we" really change anything about the dangers of this powerful reality of the modern post-industrial age?

The industrial complex is not limited to the military. We can easily identify symptoms of the corporatist virus all around us:

- Large corporations successfully lobby the government.

- The rich get richer and the wealth gap grows.

- Favors are given to campaign contributors.

- Public agencies are run like businesses.

- People in power receive perks from large corporations.

The _____ (military, agricultural, pharmaceutical, etc.) industrial complex is a concept that has great importance for people who are searching for knowledge in their decision making, particularly investment decision making. As we seek to make the best decisions in all aspects of life, we must be aware that this corporatist dynamic is ever present. The products, services, and politicians that we confront are all components of the corporatist system.

Our democracy in the United States has become dominated by a growing virus of corporatism. Corporatism is a system in which power is given or attained by civic assemblies that represent economic, industrial, financial, and many other types of groups. In my lifetime, I have witnessed an investment landscape that grows ever more complex and difficult to understand. The laws, products, and trends are, more and more often, driven by complex government legislation created in an atmosphere of intensive lobbying. The complex system that creates our economic future is increasingly structured to favor the interests of large financial, agricultural, and military conglomerates. As investors, we must be constantly vigilant and aware that this is a corporatist system and that it is often counter to the interests of the individual.

Many authors have written about this political trend, including Paul Ormerod, John Pilger, and Noam Chomsky. As investors, we must be wary of how this reality affects every opportunity and decision that is made. The financial-industrial complex will challenge investors at every step of their investment lifetime. All of the strategies, tactics, and thinking of investors must be calibrated while recognizing the shadow that corporatism casts.

This corporatist trend seems to only grow and expand with time. The expanding complexity of our laws, the Internal Revenue Code (IRC), and the regulatory environment create a landscape where structural business advantages via lobbying and political influence are more important than competition for and development of greater quality in financial products. A great example of this is the current IRC provision for what is known as a 529 college savings plan. Each state has its own plan, with great variation in quality and cost structure. There would be greater quality and economy of scale through creation of a uniform federal standard that could then be available to anyone in the United States.

401(k) plans are another dramatic example of how the complex nature of our tax law drives hundreds of billions of dollars into certain types of financial products for no other reason than the advantages of a tax law. Our entire retirement future in the United States is now based on this concept, which is completely unproven in terms of creating sufficient retirement funding for workers.

Corporatism is also reflected in the dramatic disparity in pay between the average worker and chief executive officers (CEOs) and other high-ranking executives of American corporations. A statistic that demonstrates this power of the elites is the pay gap between the CEO and the average worker in the United States. This gap has been expanding at a rapid rate according to the US Bureau of Labor Statistics. In 1990, CEO pay was 85 times that of workers. By 1999, the gap had increased to 419 times the averages worker's pay. In 2007, the gap was back down to 364 times the average pay of workers according to the annual survey, Executive Excess 2007, by the Institute for Policy Studies. This added up to an average $10.8 million in total compensation.

The growing disparity between the rich and poor is another troubling symptom of the corporatist shadow in this country. The "wealth gap" refers to the differential in the distribution of economic assets

3

and income. The wealth gap is another term for wealth inequality among groups. It has been estimated that the wealthiest 1 percent of Americans controls more the 30 percent of all the wealth in the United States. Data also suggest that this gap has been growing over the last 40 years.

It is difficult to gather accurate data on the actual breakdown of wealth in America. The Federal Reserve Board (Fed) conducts a Survey of Consumer Finances, which attempts to quantify all sorts of census data. The most recent survey data available are from 2004, although another survey is due to be released in the spring of 2009. These surveys are complicated and difficult to distill. However, many experts agree that the middle class has not been keeping pace with wages and wealth accumulation in recent decades.

Many industry examples of this "complex" influence in the modern capitalist American economy are easier to recognize than those of the financial sector. Look to agriculture as an example. As this crucial industry expands its interests with growing farm bill subsidies and lobbying, and a drastically outgunned and understaffed Food and Drug Administration, what do we see as consumers? Mass marketing efforts with relentless repetition, proliferation of fast foods, obesity, and producers inventing foods that no one really needs.

What about the quality of the end product that makes up the American diet? Does the agribusiness complex in the US continue to innovate to create healthier, more wholesome foods for the consumer? No, the modern American food supply providers seem to be doing mostly the opposite. The proliferation fast-food restaurants is a sad commentary on what the agribusiness complex has wrought on society. With a brief visit to a local mall, we can observe the trend toward obesity and unhealthy eating habits on the part of Americans. I am a great believer in individual responsibility, but it becomes ever more difficult to make rational choices in what we consume in the face of menus driven by the agribusiness complex of the US. (*The Omnivore's Dilemma*, by Michael Pollan, is a terrific starting point for learning about the modern food supply in the United States.)

Today, the US economy is experiencing food inflation not seen since the 1970s. Many point to ethanol as one of the important factors behind the food inflation of 2008. If Congress were truly interested in ethanol as a substitute for petroleum, why would it impose import tariffs on sugar-based ethanol? Large energy corporations, along with corn-producing states, are the real policymaking force behind this legislative curtain. Many commentators today are arguing that mass production of ethanol is completely energy inefficient and unsustainable. The agriculture and military complexes are creating the future as we individuals try to live quality lives. Each of us needs to recognize these forces and make important life choices in recognition of this fact.

Why did so many of us choose to purchase and drive huge SUVs and other types of energy-wasting vehicles? Is it what we demanded, or were these gas guzzlers a working example of buying what is being sold? This is a graphic example of the power of the automotive complex reaping great profit while it could, at the obvious expense of the middle and long term. The American auto manufacturers have fought mileage standards for years. The car companies have harnessed us with a transportation model that was predicated on cheap petroleum energy. The energy crisis of 2008 is a great opportunity for consumers to wake up and make choices that are sustainable in a growing world.

The unstable nature of petroleum-producing countries has been with us since the dawn of the industrial age. How is it that this great country was caught up with our entire economy being sapped by an ever increasing energy tax? We as consumers need to demand that a "Manhattan Project" for sustainable, environmentally neutral energy be commenced. Our country and its diverse population are certainly capable of innovation at the highest level. We must begin to adjust our decisions in this light. Informed and broad-minded decision making is important, and each and every consumer represents the first step to better lives and a better country. Consumer knowledge and sophistication can lead market forces that will shape a sustainable future much more efficiently than waiting for a federal energy policy to solve the challenges we currently face.

So many parts of our lives are now structured and dominated by "complex" systems that one could become a bit paranoid; we need to remember that the beauty of the human spirit is of utmost importance. We must live and navigate our decisions with as much awareness as possible of the underlying dynamics that shape our options as citizens and consumers in this great nation. The powerful antidote to this corporatist virus is education, information, and consistent rational behavior. The American citizen has a responsibility in this complex world for disciplined and informed decision making. The alternative is a world where your government, with the help of mega corporations, will make decisions for you.

Before I focus on our financial system, I would like to point out that the complex systems in our society become more numerous every day. Our pharmaceutical industry recently was granted an entire new section of Medicare called "Part D." Where do changes like this come from? Who is looking out for you as the massive force of lobbyists and lawyers grind out the legislation that emerges from Congress? The complexity of Medicare was already at an astounding level when our federal government decided to create an entirely new "drug benefit." The name of the game is lobbying for laws that create structural advantage to specific industries. Intricate IRC changes can create great windfalls for certain corporations, while putting others at a significant disadvantage. The reviews and reaction to Medicare Part D have been greatly mixed and confusion on the part of consumers has been high.

The notion that our government can actually create a drug benefit through legislative magic is questionable. These government mandates are incredibly complicated. They create huge advantages for the largest corporations, which have the resources to decipher and capitalize on the thousands of pages of arcane provisions of these laws. Take a quick trip to www.medicare.gov/pdphome.asp and go for a surf. The complexity of these rules creates a massive bureaucracy that only increases costs for all of us.

The intricate nature of Part D can be illustrated by the concept of drug "formularies." The problem is that all the Part D plans available have different benefit equations based on what drug you may take. Each state also has different rate structures. If you move to a different state and go on a new drug treatment, you may have to enroll in a different plan. This makes it all overwhelming, if not completely impossible, for our senior citizens to stay current year after year.

The financial-industrial complex is a great threat to Americans and their efforts to grow financial strength and security. It is a dark force that possesses great power. Financial-sector firms begin to take on a role that is extremely powerful and difficult for consumers to assess. The products and services that are marketed are created more in the interests of the financial industry than in the interests of consumers. Financial products are generally long term in nature and can take many years before revealing their true merit. A product milieu that is ever more complex and cryptic does not bode well for savers and investors.

The Pension Protection Act of 2006 is a frightening example of what is produced every few years by the legislature of the United States. This massive document (numbering more than 300 pages in the downloaded format that I have examined) is so complex that one has to wonder how much time and money will be spent on efforts of interpretation. It is in the complexity of these types of government decrees that the financial-industrial complex increases its influence and creates opportunities out of thin air.

Few of us could ever have the expertise, patience, and motivation required to follow and understand just what is accomplished through these mountains of complex governmental rules and regulations. I have excerpted a part of the legislation regarding investment advice below. See if you can make any sense of it without hiring a special lawyer to read it for you …

TITLE VI--INVESTMENT ADVICE, PROHIBITED TRANSACTIONS, AND FIDUCIARY

RULES

Subtitle A--Investment Advice

SEC. 601. PROHIBITED TRANSACTION EXEMPTION FOR PROVISION OF INVESTMENT

ADVICE.

(a) Amendments to the Employee Retirement Income Security Act of 1974.--

(1) Exemption from prohibited transactions.--Section 408(b) of the Employee Retirement Income Security Act of 1974 (29 U.S.C. 1108(b)) is amended by adding at the end the following new paragraph:

[[Page 120 STAT. 953]]

(14) Any transaction in connection with the provision of investment advice described in section 3(21)(A)(ii) to a participant or beneficiary of an individual account plan that permits such participant or beneficiary to direct the investment of assets in their individual account, if--

(A) the transaction is--

(i) the provision of the investment advice to the participant or beneficiary of the plan with respect to a security or other property available as an investment under the plan,

(ii) the acquisition, holding, or sale of a security or other property available as an investment under the plan pursuant to the investment advice, or

(iii) the direct or indirect receipt of fees or other compensation by the fiduciary adviser or an affiliate thereof (or any employee, agent, or

registered representative of the fiduciary adviser

or affiliate) in connection with the provision of

the advice or in connection with an acquisition,

holding, or sale of a security or other property

available as an investment under the plan pursuant

to the investment advice; and

(B) the requirements of subsection (g) are met.

(2) Requirements.--Section 408 of such Act <<NOTE: 29 USC

1108.>> is amended further by adding at the end the following

new subsection:

(g) Provision of Investment Advice to Participant and

Beneficiaries.--

(1) In general.--The prohibitions provided in section 406

shall not apply to transactions described in subsection (b)(14)

if the investment advice provided by a fiduciary adviser is

provided under an eligible investment advice arrangement.

(2) Eligible investment advice arrangement.--For purposes

of this subsection, the term `eligible investment advice

arrangement' means an arrangement--

(A) which either--

(i) provides that any fees (including any

commission or other compensation) received by the

fiduciary adviser for investment advice or with

respect to the sale, holding, or acquisition of

any security or other property for purposes of

investment of plan assets do not vary depending on

the basis of any investment option selected, or

(ii) uses a computer model under an

investment advice program meeting the requirements

of paragraph (3) in connection with the provision

of investment advice by a fiduciary adviser to a

participant or beneficiary, and

(B) with respect to which the requirements of

paragraph (4), (5), (6), (7), (8), and (9) are met.

(3) Investment advice program using computer model.--

(A) In general.--An investment advice program

meets the requirements of this paragraph if the

requirements of subparagraphs (B), (C), and (D) are met.

(B) Computer model.--The requirements of this

subparagraph are met if the investment advice provided

[[Page 120 STAT. 954]]

under the investment advice program is provided pursuant

to a computer model that--

(i) applies generally accepted investment theories that take into account the historic returns of different asset classes over defined periods of time,

(ii) utilizes relevant information about the participant, which may include age, life expectancy, retirement age, risk tolerance, other assets or sources of income, and preferences as to certain types of investments,

(iii) utilizes prescribed objective criteria to provide asset allocation portfolios comprised of investment options available under the plan,

(iv) operates in a manner that is not biased in favor of investments offered by the fiduciary adviser or a person with a material affiliation or contractual relationship with the fiduciary adviser, and

(v) takes into account all investment options under the plan in specifying how a participant's account balance should be invested and is not inappropriately weighted with respect to any investment option.

(C) Certification.--

(i) In general.--The requirements of this subparagraph are met with respect to any investment advice program if an eligible investment expert certifies, prior to the utilization of the computer model and in accordance with rules prescribed by the Secretary, that the computer model meets the requirements of subparagraph (B).

(ii) Renewal of certifications.--If, as determined under regulations prescribed by the Secretary, there are material modifications to a computer model, the requirements of this subparagraph are met only if a certification described in clause (i) is obtained with respect to the computer model as so modified.

(iii) Eligible investment expert.--The term `eligible investment expert' means any person--

(I) which meets such requirements as the Secretary may provide, and

(II) does not bear any material affiliation or contractual relationship with any investment adviser or a related

person thereof (or any employee, agent,

or registered representative of the

investment adviser or related person).

(D) Exclusivity of recommendation.--The

requirements of this subparagraph are met with respect

to any investment advice program if--

(i) the only investment advice provided

under the program is the advice generated by the

computer model described in subparagraph (B), and

(ii) any transaction described in subsection

(b)(14)(B)(ii) occurs solely at the direction of

the participant or beneficiary.

Nothing in the preceding sentence shall preclude the

participant or beneficiary from requesting investment

advice other than that described in subparagraph (A).

Somewhere in the above word salad, I think there is language that makes it legal for retirement plans, including the ubiquitous 401(k) plan, to offer the participants advice that they can pay for. Many overwhelming questions are raised by these governmental documents. Has anyone actually ever tried to read them? Who are the actual authors? Who are the winners and who are the losers?

It is disheartening to see the actual details in these types of government documents, which are produced with regularity. The process of creating this endless stream of legislation is at the heart of the power of the financial-industrial complex. It is incumbent upon US citizens to become actively informed and not to leave our interests in the hands of lawyers, politicians, and lobbyists.

As a practicing advisor, I have found that many retirement plan participants are in need of guidance and ongoing advice. The group 401(k) faces challenges as to how to deliver guidance to the worker in a way that helps the worker to make rational choices. I have been perplexed by what I can actually do for plan participants under the law. As legislation from 1974 and 1986, and now 2006, bear down on those workers that need guidance, it is increasingly difficult to discern what is actually permissible and what is not. New rules overwrite older rules constantly and it is extremely challenging to stay current. It becomes difficult to know what can and cannot be done legally as a practicing financial advisor for 401(k) participants.

Consumers can shape this emerging world run by and for corporations. The first step is one of education and understanding that our American standard of living is not guaranteed. The greatest way to ensure a positive future for our descendents is through education and the rational choices we make. Proactive behavior is extremely important. Those who proceed passively will be at risk for disappointment, and worse.

There are many "complex" forces in the USA, but this dynamic is part and parcel to the globalization movement that emerged in the early 1980s. Our decisions as voters, consumers, and human beings have a significant global impact. I want to proceed into this discussion of "complex corporatism" with a focus on financial matters and the financial-industrial complex, and the role that we can play as intelligent actors in our own interests.

This financial-industrial complex disaster is built on a platform of which most of us will never be aware. The difference between an efficient, quality financial product and one that is 1 percent or 2 percent less good is not very obvious until we measure it over time. The compounding of excess costs or poor-quality management can end up claiming a dramatic amount of an investor's ultimate value. The players in this financial-industrial complex comprise a long list. Below I delineate some of the industry participants that we need to be aware of.

The mutual fund industry has accumulated more than $12 trillion as of year-end 2007, according to the website of the Investment Company Institute. This sector was anointed back in 1978 when section 401(k) of the IRC was developed. Your future retirement income will be shaped by the products of this group of companies.

The Internal Revenue Service (IRS) is not just your tax collector. The changes to the IRC provide a golden opportunity for financial companies to create windfall profits based on IRS decree.

The banking/lending industry is the creator of the current mortgage and housing crisis. This reflects a sad transformation from the days when a bank actually cared that a loan it made was likely to be repaid. Securitization of lending is a complex process where the many mortgage lenders are simply marketers of money, who then sell loans to Wall Street and move on to the next transaction.

The Fed has a stated mission created by the Federal Reserve Act of 1913. The mission is "to provide for the establishment of Federal Reserve Banks, to furnish an elastic currency, to afford means of rediscounting commercial paper, to establish a more effective supervision of banking in the United States, and for other purposes." Essentially, the Fed sets interest rates and controls the money supply. The decisions made at the Fed have massive global impact on economic growth and inflation.

The insurance industry is a critical component to almost all forms of commerce in our capitalist system. In a corporatist world, the insurance industry consistently ranks among the top 10 in amounts given to Congress. New insurance business can be created overnight by Congress and the IRS, and in their continued quest for growth, insurance companies have touched almost every transaction we can enter. From insurance on your new toaster to insurance against specific diseases, one must be constantly vigilant to discern what premiums are actually worth paying for protection from real insurable risk.

Financial regulators (i.e., Financial Industry Regulatory Authority, Securities and Exchange Commission, Office of the Comptroller of the Currency, et al.) are faced with the overwhelming task of enforcing the laws and regulations that are continuously becoming more complex. Generally, regulators are underfunded and outmatched by the financial-industrial complex. Most bureaucrats serve a limited number of years in service to the government before moving into the private sector, where the financial rewards are significantly higher.

Accountants and the Financial Accounting Standards Board are charged with the task of honest and transparent reporting of corporations and all forms of enterprise in the United States. Unfortunately, the accounting profession has developed the concept of "business consulting" due to the fact that recordkeeping and reporting is a low-growth, commodity business. Huge conflicts of interest are created when an accounting firm also provides consulting services. Enron is the poster child for this sad dynamic (see *Conspiracy of Fools*, by Kurt Eichenwald).

This list could go on and on. Many forces work below the surface to constantly wrangle for advantage. The final products we see in the marketplace should be evaluated with skepticism. It may be impossible to understand the forces that shape our world, but we need to be aware of what is out there. My aim in writing this book is to document all that I have learned and continue to use in my thinking as a professional advisor and investor. Our behavior as investors and consumers of financial products can have a lasting impact in the face of this corporatist world.

A passion for investing, and the great benefits of financial strength and security that it can bring, is what I have pursued for a great portion of my life. The goal should not be wealth or riches, but rather the maximization of each and every person's means, so that all people can reach their individual potential. Education is the great opportunity in so many ways, beyond raising our career, academic, or professional potential. If we can all make more informed and rational choices, the world can change for the better. There are no great secrets contained in the chapters that comprise this book, only reinforcement of the fundamentals of sound financial decision making that over time will lead to financial strength, security, and confidence.

This book has been written to begin a discussion of the fundamentals that all investors must consider in light of the complex system that presents all of us with choices. Seeing the world as it is, and proceeding accordingly with an outlook that seeks fundamental information and truth, is the way that we can all protect and strengthen our present lives and future possibilities. No one person will ever have the power to stop the progress of the financial-industrial complex. The reality of the modern world will only be improved if all of us make better decisions on a day-to-day basis and over the middle and long run.

The place to begin this pursuit of financial knowledge is at the most fundamental level—that is, the critical distinction between owning things and loaning money to earn interest. Let us reduce our basic choices to this most fundamental level. The complexity that exists does not need to inhibit the pursuit of basic knowledge of how things work. The long-term impact of this difference between loaning and owning is shocking. Let us now proceed to discussing and learning about the two ways that money can work for all of us to create financial strength over time.

Behavioral Economics

"Economics is extremely useful as a form of employment for economists."

John Kenneth Galbraith

During my time as a student, I had two main interests, economics and psychology. I spent endless hours contemplating serious economic concepts of supply and demand, gross domestic product (GDP), gross national product (GNP), and interest rates; I read and thought about personality types, phobias, and all the problems and challenges of human psychology.

In my youthful and idealistic state of mind, I felt certain that the very essence of financial truth and success must be found in the wisdom that economists held in their brains. The beauty of supply and demand theories was alluring to me. The path to success and wealth seemed to be paved with economic theories of rational individuals acting in their best interests. But, this idealism ignores the huge impact of human irrationality! In the real world, most of us do not make rational decisions with much consistency vis-à-vis our financial dilemmas. I have learned over time that scientific models cannot explain much of what happens. You do not have to search very hard to find stark examples of dramatic human irrationality—from drug abuse to war, from junk food to the fad of piercing various body parts. The most important lessons I learned as an investor were not picked up in economics and business classes, but, rather, in the school of psychology!

To see the world in a way that is more realistic than mathematical economic and finance models would suggest, a branch of economics that takes human behavior into consideration has developed. The merging of economics and psychology is known as behavioral economics, or behavioral finance. Daniel Kahneman won the Nobel Prize in 2002 for groundbreaking work in this emerging branch of academia. This field looks to study an economic world filled with real humans, not intelligent computer-generated agents that populate economic models and theories. Behavior-based models and theories recognize that people often act in ways that seem and may actually be quite irrational. This is easy to believe when we look at the scandals, panics, and wars that continue to plague the modern world.

It is important for all investors to be aware of the concepts that behavioral economics and finance are beginning to research and study. Let us take a look at a few of the most important built-in defects or cognitive biases that we have as humans/investors.

"Confirmation bias" is the human tendency to interpret information in a way that confirms one's outlook or preconceptions. People tend to avoid information and interpretations that contradict their prior beliefs. Peter C. Wason studied this dynamic in 1960. His research showed that people tend only to think about proving a theory, without doing equal work on disproving it or searching for what may not be known. A humorous Murphy's Law supports this concept: "Enough research will tend to support your theory."

I often see this lack of acceptance of counter evidence when investors are confronted with information regarding high costs or mediocre performance of long-held investments. Many times, John Q. Investor will say, "My broker Bill is a great guy, and he has always done great for me," even though Bill has never offered any long-term measurement or comparison of the investments. The common mindset seems to be one that is disinterested in negative or critical information.

A powerful example of this is an institution that is perceived as "liberal," such as the *New York Times*. Many of those who consider themselves politically conservative simply will not accept information or opinion from a source that is defined as left wing. However, as rational investors, we must pursue many varied sources of information to avoid seeing only the facts that support our theories.

The lesson here for investors may be the most critical of all. We have a predisposition to seek information that is consistent with what we already believe. I often think that this is at the root of many of the world's great military and humanitarian disasters. Just imagine if the great leaders of our world could step back and really weigh all sides of the decision process without pressure from those forces that would benefit from military conflict. Maybe we could even have regulation on the production of weaponry for profit. Imagine a world where no companies could reap windfall gains when there was a military conflict. Maybe then our leaders could look at the many sides of the proposition of war with scientific objectivity.

We must make our financial decisions with a keen awareness of this lack of objectivity in our brain function. This natural human stubbornness may be one of the greatest causes of poor decision making in all types of financial situations. People tend to cling to what they know for a variety of poor reasons, but confirmation bias is a proven dynamic that must be recognized with the greatest of respect.

"Short-term bias" or, more precisely, "hyperbolic discounting" occurs when people overemphasize their immediate desires. This human tendency to prefer smaller payoffs now over larger payoffs later has been proven by many psychological scholars (Green et. al., 1994; Kirby, 1997). "Eat, drink, and be merry, for tomorrow we may die" may have been a reasonable proposition for warriors before a battle in the Middle Ages, but for investors this is the path to ruin. It is a bias that has been hardwired into our human brain function. As people succumb to their preference for immediate gratification, they risk the middle and long run by not consistently saving enough to create longer term security and strength.

Another scientific term for this is "temporal myopia." This is the difficulty the human brain has in understanding the distance of time. The further something is in the future, the less relevance it has to the human brain. This dynamic is related to dysfunctional behaviors beyond investing and money management. We all must be wary of this built-in bias that contributes to so many of the difficult problems modern man faces, like procrastination, drug addiction, and unsafe sex. I believe this human failing destines many to live only for the short term, with little financial security as they age.

"Risk aversion" is the tendency for investors to settle for lower potential return in exchange for more predictable outcomes. If an investor is overly concerned about short-term losses, his or her investment strategy will gravitate toward loss minimization and never produce the necessary return to achieve long-term compounding. I often see this desire for security exploited by financial salespeople and marketing firms that make claims about "safety" while never discussing long-term erosion of purchasing power and other risks that are created when an investor allocates investments too conservatively.

"Inappropriate extrapolation" occurs when we are overly influenced by recent events. The current oil and commodity price shock of 2008 is causing investors to feel that the future is grim due to rising costs and falling supply of global natural resources. A more rational long-term investor might reason that human innovation will always solve these seemingly dire problems and see today's environment as a great investing opportunity now that stock prices are lower due to these short-term fears.

A recent development I have noticed along this line of short-term bias is the television concept of promoting "breaking news" as something you should be excited about. The financial news outlets are promoting "exclusive" and "breaking" stories as if you could actually take this information and make trades that would be profitable because you learned that something was happening and acted on it quickly. An investor who is fully aware of the tendency of the human brain to overweight recent events will be able to resist the urge to react and stay patient and long-term minded.

"Overconfidence" is the other side of risk aversion. This is an evolutionary bias in the human brain that allows those who are very confident or even grandiose to survive and even accomplish great things. Without the visionary humans who saw beyond the limitations of their primitive world, we might have never existed. For the investor in the complex modern world, humility in assessing one's abilities to make investing decisions is much more valuable. Often, I see this when markets are down for a 9- or 12-month stretch and I begin to get calls from investors making dire market predictions that things will get worse and they should sell now. These individuals are suddenly overconfident (and risk averse now that the market is in a down cycle) that they can make the right move based on knowledge of the current panic du jour. These people have suddenly become (amateur) market timers! We must continuously remain humble to understand that our ability to predict or time the market is quite limited or completely nonexistent.

"Fear of regret" is a powerful bias toward the status quo. We often feel it is better to make no decision rather than regret a wrong decision later. This is often exhibited in investors who have held a losing investment for years and are afraid to sell before the recovery comes. Making change to an investment strategy is never easy, but once the facts of a particular strategy have been carefully considered, we must proceed with an understanding that regret is always possible. Regret is a natural part of the life and investing decision process, not something that needs to be feared.

This dynamic can cause irrational behavior when we do not follow a given recommendation that proves to be a missed opportunity. Take the example of someone who was given a stock recommendation, but never purchased the stock which then proceeded to go up in value. The next time a "tip" is received, that investor may dive in recklessly, motivated by the regret of missing the first opportunity.

As I approach this mission of delineating my philosophy and theory of living a healthy financial life, I want to emphasize that we must see the questions through this prism of irrationality. A basic understanding of the cognitive biases that have evolved into the modern human brain is extremely helpful in avoiding the lure of instincts that can trump rationality. The sequence of decisions that create our life story will be filled with trade-offs and with many questions for which there is no "right" answer. Often, decisions may be rational in the short term, but not in the middle or long term. Our desire to create security today may hinder our long-term best interests.

This is often the behavior of investors as they struggle to cope with down markets and the inevitable declines through which successful investors must persevere. People will become completely fixated on the "loss" they have suffered and make irrational statements and decisions based on their interpretation of that decline. During down markets,

I hear the same things over and over, as if people are reading from a script that they have all rehearsed for the same performance: "I can't afford to lose" and "I lost more this year than I added this year" are chanted like mantras. But, as investors, the key to success is to ensure that our portfolio is properly allocated and placed in quality assets with money managers who have track records of success, not to concentrate on the direction of the market in any given year. This type of objective analysis and long-term thinking is extremely difficult during uncertain economic times.

Many "experts" and commentators communicate and publish materials that profess to lay out blueprints and techniques for financial success. Books on personal finance filled with wonderful and useful information have been available for years. Why is it then that so many of us are stranded in a state of insecurity? Numerous families seem to live from paycheck to paycheck. The low savings rate and financial ignorance that I see as a practicing financial advisor is clear evidence to me that the information in books will actually help very few, if any, people. It is not knowledge of rational strategy, but our behavior that will ultimately determine the financial outcome of our lives.

Look again at the current day and you will find a massive example of how this irrationality plagues the US and most developed nations. In 2008, you would be rational to assume that the act of taking debt for one's personal residence would be a fairly evolved science. Home ownership and property rights are one of the cornerstones of modern American capitalism. Apparently, however, mortgage lending is not quite a science. Judging by the current crisis, it sure seems like there has been quite a chain of errors.

The current environment has accumulated numerous labels since the third quarter of 2007 when the sub-prime/housing/mortgage crisis began to be revealed. Whatever you call it, it is useful for learning about the dangers of financial engineering and the vulnerability of the investing masses in their decision making. The chain of events and decisions that have led to so much pain is truly fascinating. Why would lenders not demand documentation of income before issuing mortgages? Who are the people who recklessly overbought or overbuilt their homes beyond any reasonable ability to afford the cost? Why does our culture seem to demand so much more (in this case, of super large homes) than we could ever need? Look to behavioral finance to begin to investigate why!

The economic principles we need to learn are simple and straightforward. Sophisticated economic knowledge is not required, nor do I believe that economic experts are destined to get rich. Financial strength is a direct result of behavior. Changing our habits and ways of thinking is a huge challenge. It is analogous to keeping the weight off after the crash diet to lose 20 pounds. Losing the weight is the easy part … keeping it off may be impossible! We must be able to continuously make healthy eating decisions over our lifetime, not just follow a diet protocol to lose weight. Our short-term bias toward chocolate cake must be overcome on an ongoing basis.

To become financially strong, you need a set of principles, not a diet. Discipline, patience, and belief in the importance of the middle and long run are critical to investors who seek efficient growth of their money. Sacrificing satisfaction today for benefits in our future is one of the most difficult things we can do. You must recognize this fact. There are endless short-term temptations that will present you with short-term pleasure and long-term pain. Borrowing against one's home at the risk to future security is an ever repeating example of this. People are constantly convincing themselves (or lying to themselves, to satisfy the short-term cravings) that they can spend now and work things out later.

Another great example is the proliferation of fast-food outlets, a graphic symbol of short-term thinking and poor decision making. Would rational people really demand so much unhealthy fat-laden food? I think the food supply here in the US is a powerful example of how we have all been led astray by marketing and over-processing that exploits the natural human tendency for wanting what we want … now!

How else can you explain the mass consumption of cigarettes, liquor, and unhealthy food? Ironically, our culture has evolved in the direction of consumption versus discipline and fitness. The free market continuously seeks to separate people from their money. Rapid gratification has engulfed our way of life, from drive-through food and banking to "instant" lotteries (gambling right at your local grocery store, how convenient is that?!).

Las Vegas is the modern monument to our human lust for short-term gratification at the expense of our overall best interests. It is fascinating to think that this desert town had such a colossal impact on American culture by allowing legalized gambling on March 19, 1931. The gambling era of Las Vegas was actually founded by organized crime figures Bugsy Siegel and Meyer Lansky. The impact of this after 80 years is astounding to contemplate. We now have legalized gambling in various forms throughout the United States, and this legacy has its origins in organized crime! I find it ironic when I see politicians marketing themselves as those who possess high moral values, juxtaposed against a landscape increasingly infiltrated by the gambling industry.

Whatever moral view you may hold about gambling or "gaming," as it has now been re-branded, no one can deny that it is a troubling example of the financial ignorance of our population. It is not difficult to learn about the advantage of the house in all casino games and the impossibility of gains from participation in such games. Yet our culture is producing an increasing stream of gamblers seeking short-term thrills and willing to pay for the growing spectacle that is Vegas. This modern gabling culture may be the most powerful symbol of our short-term fixation. We must constantly be vigilant against these tendencies in order to promote long-term financial health. When planning how to spend our time, it is important to not only consider the excitement of the fancy vacation, but also the long plane ride home, with a wallet that is likely much lighter than when we left.

When a person embarks on a life journey that has the constant goal of financial fitness, one must remember that the environment and culture is stacked against a positive outcome. The siren temptation of spending, shoddy investments, "common" wisdom that does more harm than good, and various other factors are lurking around every corner. I cannot emphasize enough that investing is not like most other things. When we make financial decisions, mistakes may only become apparent much later. A bad pizza or a lousy bicycle will be obvious and we can adjust our preferences to avoid those companies in the future. If, on the other hand, we are too conservative or misguided in our investment decisions, we may never realize it until it is too late.

Our behavior is also guided by survival instincts. An area of interest to me as an advisor is how we are all affected so greatly by fear. When an investment begins to fall in value, the natural human reaction is to sell and wait for "better times." I am always amazed that certain clients, who rarely call me, are ringing my phone off the hook after one bad quarter. The moment many investors see declines on a quarterly statement, they immediately think that something is wrong. I often tease by saying … Why didn't you call me when your account went up?

The dynamic here is that the human brain is approximately three times more sensitive to loss than it is appreciative of gain. We are happy to make money, but there is great despair in the face of a decline. It is likely that the thousands of years that man evolved living from one meal to the next has a lot to do with this irrationality. Think about it, imagine the caveman wondering where he would find his next meal. These emotions are embedded deeply in our conscious and subconscious.

People need to understand the concept of "good investment, bad market." In my study of mutual funds with track records of more than 30 years, I have found some powerful statistics. One of the most powerful is that when you measure results over 12- month periods, you will find that about one of every three years is negative! We need to prepare our investor mind for the reality that there will be a lot of down years where we will have to weather storms. If you measure over the average five-year period, the results are positive nearly 90 percent of the time! Most comfortingly, most 10-year periods are positive. One year does not an investment make. We must constantly remind our brains of this fact.

The Two Ways That Money Works

"Rather than love, than money, than fame, give me truth."

Henry David Thoreau

When an investor contemplates putting money to work, there are endless choices. It can be overwhelming for even the most sophisticated individuals to filter through all the variations. An incomplete list will include stocks, bonds, mutual funds, real estate investment trusts (REITs), whole life insurance, unit trusts, exchange-traded funds (ETFs), limited partnerships, annuities, hedge funds, private equity, and venture capital. We could spend a good portion of our investing life grinding through an initial examination of the different investment vehicles. Most of the complicated offerings that are produced by financial marketing firms should be cast aside. Look for the very essence of what is important first, and then the selection process can become easier.

Analyzing the components of ocean water is not necessary if you are deciding to go for a swim, although you may want to check for riptides, sharks, and jellyfish. Most of us will be able to dive in without ever considering any of the scientific or oceanographic minutiae. Financial product complexity will stop many from ever taking money from the bank and putting it to work. This is and will likely be the greatest mistake made by a large portion of the population. Things do not have to be complicated. If we can demystify the process of properly employing our money, it will become as natural as going for a swim in beautiful, warm, calm ocean waters. With this understanding, we can take the first step to becoming an informed, prudent investor.

The simple reality is that there are only two choices: You can be either an owner or a loaner. Every investment made will fall into one of these two categories. Let's make it simple (because what we need to know is simple).

<u>Loaner</u>	<u>Owner</u>
Bonds	Stock
Debt	Equity
Fixed Investments	Variable Investments
Guaranteed Returns	Unknown Returns
Historical Average 6%	Historical Average 10%

I often hear people say, "Oh yeah, stocks and bonds … that stuff is too scary for me … I am not a gambler." But, the fundamental decision we all face is that an investor can decide to:

- Buy stakes of ownership, or

- Be a lender of capital.

This is the decision that we must make with complete understanding. Stocks and bonds should not even be referred to in the same sentence. It is the contrast between the North Pole and the equator, as different as the merchant owner and the janitor who cleans the store.

Let us look at this graphically:

OWNERSHIP   LOANERSHIP

????   %%%%

The graphic above hugely oversimplifies yet clarifies our decision. The owner can only wonder about future results. The loaner/lender can have complete certainty of the rate of return for the term of the investment.

Bonds (loaner choice) are contracts that obligate the issuer to pay holders of a debt interest (the coupon) on a stated schedule. At a contractual maturity date, the borrower is then obligated to repay the principal. If the bond issuer does not repay on schedule, the bond owner may have claim to assets that could be liquidated. A bond is simply a loan, but in the form of a security.

Stock typically takes the form of shares of common stock. As a unit of ownership, common stock typically carries voting rights that can be exercised in corporate decisions.

Bonds and stock are not part of the same realm. They are as different as night and day, air and water, and passive and assertive.

There are endless variations of fixed (bond) and variable (stock) investments. There are also hybrid instruments that contain both owner and loaner characteristics. I believe that most people simply do not understand the fundamental distinction and, thus, can never make rational saving and investing decisions.

Let us think about decisions that an investor may have to face in a simple hypothetical scenario. XYZ Company is a new software company that is raising money to fuel its efforts to grow and exploit profit opportunities. What options does it have to raise this money? XYZ can borrow (loan) or sell stock (ownership). Those are the only two options. There are many variations on this choice: bonds or bank loans, venture capital, private placements, and an initial public offering. But let's leave those issues to the pros and sharks in New York City, London, and Silicon Valley. Let us simply consider the choice that all investors face—whether to own assets for appreciation or lend money and earn interest along with security of principal through repossession if the company should go under.

Now, how does this basic relationship play out for the investor? The investor who is going to loan money to XYZ is going to get a stated rate of interest on that money. The rate could actually be very high because XYZ is a new company and it may fail to survive. The lender here may actually be taking a high risk to offer funds for a loan agreement. In fact, XYZ may not even be able to borrow due to the high risk of default (but let's keep this simple). So, we go ahead and buy an XYZ bond with a coupon of 12 percent. Wow, that sounds great! I get my 12 percent interest every year (paid semiannually), and if XYZ goes bust, I will have a claim on its building or other assets that it bought with the money that I lent.

The claim on actual assets is what makes the bond a fixed investment that carries a lower level of risk to the investor's principal. If for some reason XYZ goes out of business, I will get some or all of my original investment back when the assets or real estate of whatever XYZ owned is auctioned off in bankruptcy.

The alternative is for the investor who wants to be an owner in XYZ. There will be no monthly payments and no certainty here. With no guaranteed percentage of interest per year on our investment, our return is an unknown. If XYZ goes on to grow and prosper, my share of ownership can expand greatly in value, possibly bringing a return of much more than the 12 percent in the bond offering. But, if XYZ does go bust, my entire ownership investment will most likely be lost.

The investment outcome here is not the point, but comprehending this choice between the two structures for our money is the most critical distinction we make. Those who do not recognize this difference are at a disadvantage due to ignorance of the fundamental difference between stocks (owning) and bonds (loaning). There is no need to own stakes in companies that are unproven and risky. As I will explain shortly, we can own diversified groups of established companies to help reduce the risk of ownership. The rational choice for most investors may be investments in those companies with long histories of prudent management and profit growth.

My very strong belief in the ownership principle and the foundation of my investing philosophy is that wealth is created over time through ownership of quality companies. The value of this ownership in a diversified basket of established companies has, historically, been one of the greatest creators of wealth. Conversely, loaning our money for interest creates stability of the day-to-day value of our account, but greatly reduces the opportunity for real growth over time.

Patient, disciplined owners who have held for the long term have been rewarded throughout economic history. Many large corporations can become more efficient and potentially more valuable to own over time. The warehouse chain incurs great cost to build its store, but over time those costs are absorbed. A hotel is built, and then the costs of that development are amortized and the room rental fees can roll in year after year. Human resources policies do not have to be constantly reinvented. This concept has endless examples.

There is also an economic principle here that has to do with population growth and growth in the money supply. Our world is constantly expanding as populations and new technologies proliferate. I want to avoid deep economic discussions here, but I do think that these dynamics help place an upward bias in the value of owning quality businesses over time. I have an optimistic view of our ever growing and innovating human future.

We can easily witness this wealth creation when examining rankings of the world's wealthiest people. The list is heavily weighted toward ownership. This is obviously an oversimplification, but I am ironclad in my belief that the only way to financial strength for the great majority of our wage-earning population is through the equity ownership mechanism. Most of us will never approach the level of the world's wealthiest, but we can do everything possible to emulate the choices that the richest among us make.

The investing world is filled with endless variation and complexity, but the results that we experience as investors will be determined by our understanding and allocation into the two categories of ownership and loanership. In my years of practice as a financial advisor, I have spent much of my time helping people understand this fundamental concept. Once a person can become comfortable with the notion of being an owner, the process of building financial strength over the long run can begin.

The simplification of this idea of ownership should not mask the challenge of living through market cycles, particularly when an investor sees the value of his or her holdings drop in value during a bear market. No matter how diversified a given portfolio may be, it is likely to experience periods of decline in value. These declines can be significant in the short run. During these bear markets, it is extremely difficult to see the future recovery stage, which has always occurred throughout economic history. It is also important to point out that bear market cycles can take three or even five years to recover, so we must balance our mid- and long-term investments with significant portions of secure cash reserves and bond investments. These fixed loaner investments will allow for ready cash so that we do not have to sell stocks during down market cycles.

The essential notion here is that the more wealth an investor can build using equity-based ownership, the greater the growth rates will be over time. As rational and disciplined long-term investors, we can circumvent the corporatist dangers that exist and gain the benefits that accrue to owners over time. By avoiding complex financial products that are produced and refined by the financial-industrial complex, we can seek straightforward mutual funds that can create efficient ways to own widely diversified stock portfolios.

Just as we must eat a balanced diet to maintain our physical health, we need to create a diversified portfolio, complete with lots of whole grains (ownership) and vegetables (diversification). This process will take place over the long run. It will be difficult, demanding, and, most of the time, not very exciting.

Next I explore the critical differences that loaners and owners can expect in their investment results over time.

Owners Grow, Loaners Preserve

"The individual has always had to struggle to keep from being overwhelmed by the tribe. If you try it, you will be lonely often, and sometimes frightened. But no price is too high to pay for the privilege of owning yourself."

Friedrich Nietzsche

Take a ride around town. One thing you will always see is a whole lot of … banks. Old, new, internet (you will not see the virtual banks on your drive), credit unions, savings and loans. Must be a great business to be in, right? It is.

Why is that? Go back to ECON 101 … to the chapter on banking. BORING … oh, what you missed. What is the essence of the banking business? Loans, right? Well, the bank is making money on … other people's money. The bank is not lending its own dollars. That is probably why it is so quiet and relaxed at the bank. Heck, it's not the bank's money if something goes wrong! This is a critical point in our education. Banks operate as intermediaries. Borrowing low and lending high is a business that dreams are made of. Banking may, in fact, be the greatest business known to man, or at least economic man.

The banking crisis of 2008 is another reminder of the financial-industrial complex and the consequences, intended and unintended, that periodically occur. It is clear that modern banking is currently undergoing the most severe crisis and reformation in post-Depression history. One can only hope that someday soon, banking will get back to its fundamental role in our society. Investors need to understand these fundamentals, and I find they often do not.

The bank needs a certain amount of its own capital, but, essentially, it is an intermediary. The business is based on paying Bob 5.25 percent on his five-year certificate of deposit (CD), and loaning against Betty's home purchase at 7.5 percent. Sit back and watch the profits roll in. Sounds great to me! I, as a safety-conscious investor, will gladly take the 5.25 percent risk free … let's see if it really is risk free.

Bob just got a $50,000 five-year CD at the Farmers Credit Union for 5.25 percent; what a great investment! Really? Let's see if we can simplify this. We know that Bob is a loaner. Also, Bob is guaranteed his principal by Uncle Sam. If there is ever a problem at the bank, the Federal Deposit Insurance Corporation (FDIC) would step in and pay Bob back. So there is no risk, right? Wrong!

The biggest risk will be inflation. Without bogging down in ECON 101, let's just define inflation as the fact that prices tend to go up over time. The historical average is between 2.5 percent and 3 percent. So, what is Bob's real return? Somewhere around 2.5 percent. Income tax will also take a bite every year, depending on Bob's tax bracket. But let's not be fancy or complex about this. The real result (net of inflation) will be $50,000 @ 3.25% for 5 years = $58,670.57.

Sounds good. I just saw Bob the other day and he loves his CD. He trusts his bank. It gave him a great rate on the CD, and the bank threw in a free calendar for next year and a box of cookies! Bob told me in the first five minutes that he had no desire to take risk. He only wanted to "invest" with a strong bank that would guarantee his principal. I try to educate as follows.

"Bob, having guaranteed principal is nice, but what about purchasing power and real growth? Bob, you are now 50 years old. Betty, your loving wife, is also 50. Either or both of you could easily live another 30 years. My advice is that we examine the risk to your purchasing power over the next 10, 20, and 30 years." He told me he would think about what I had said and get back to me. While I wait for Bob to call me back, let's go in a little further.

I ran some basic math using various estimates of recent returns for different types of investments. The loaner in the hypothetical scenario below holds assets in CDs at insured banks and also invests in US government bonds. The owner holds assets in a balanced mutual fund portfolio with a target of 70 percent to be allocated to stocks. Here is what I come up with …

Figure 3a

10-Year Hypothetical

Investor Allocation	Loaner	Ownership Portfolio
Average Annual Return	5.83%	8.23%
$50,000 Becomes (nominal)	$88,117	$110,267
Average Annual Return (inflation adjusted)	2.83%	5.23%
$50,000 Becomes (real growth)	$66,095	$83,246

Note the impact of inflation. Real returns estimate the impact of 3 percent inflation on the gross or nominal returns.

Figure 3b

20-Year Hypothetical

Investor Allocation	Loaner	Ownership Portfolio
Average Annual Return	7.26%	9.89%
$50,000 Becomes (nominal)	$203,107	$329,711
Average Annual Return (inflation adjusted)	4.26%	6.89%
$50,000 Becomes (real growth)	$115,166	$189,545

In the two tables above we see hypothetical investment results of the 10-year and 20-year time frames. The hypothetical loaner is a CD investor over the last 20 years. The owner investor has a combination of stocks and bonds, a common example of which is an equity income fund. These numbers are strictly hypothetical and should be used for discussion purposes only.

There are many important lessons in these simple numbers. The first issue that I emphasize is the difference between historical returns of fixed investments and equity investments. Over the 20-year time frame, the owners accumulate 40 percent more wealth!

The second critical point is the massive impact of inflation over time. Inflation takes an ever greater toll on our investment the longer the time frame that we examine. There is no magical cure for the decreasing value of money. I believe it is a natural part of capitalism. As money gets created every day by the government and by all kinds of borrowing, the value of our money is depleted over time. This is a risk that loaners do not want to think or know about. As investors, however, we must recognize that the lower the return on our investment, the greater the impact of inflation will be.

Let me expand this last point by looking again at figure 3b. Under the assumption that inflation has averaged the 3 percent used in the table, what portion is that of our total return?

For the loaner, the 3 percent inflation costs 41.33 percent of the loaner's gross return (3/7.26 = .413). Over the last 20 years, our historical Bob has been under the illusion of 7.26 percent returns. All he wants to think about is that his original $50,000 is now a bank account worth $203,107. The perception is that of safety, when in the real economic world of decreasing purchasing power, more than 40 percent of Bob's "interest" has been eaten by the beast that is inflation.

The cost of 3 percent inflation to the owner is 3/9.89 = .30. The drag of inflation is a huge toll on our results as owners, but a very significant improvement.

Lending is for banks! A bank can earn great returns on the spread between what it pays to depositors and what it charges borrowers. The bank can play a critical role for investors as a depository for short-term funds and cash management. For long-term capital appreciation, it is my position that bank saving is a costly mistake. In practice, I find that almost every time, bank savers have no understanding of this.

The last 20 years have been an era of many dramatic events and periods of great uncertainty. It is easy to look back at these long-term numbers and conclude that investing in an owner strategy was the most rational choice. Living through the ups and downs of the owner strategy was not easy during 1987, 1990, or 2002. The financial crisis of 2008 is the greatest test in many years; it is now placing possibly the highest stress on owners since the 1930s.

During down markets is when owners really make the money … by not selling in fear! Key to the ability to long-term-minded, patient investing is understanding the rewards of ownership. A diverse portfolio of blue chip stocks held over the last 50 years has returned between 10 percent and 12 percent.

To be able to hold during the periods of decline, investors must know what they own. Patient long-term investors can stay confident by looking at the reports of what stocks are held inside a given mutual fund portfolio. Mutual funds that have long track records are essential. These track records will allow investors to look back and see that during other grim economic times, long-term holders of the given fund were rewarded during the eventual recovery. The knowledge that things have generally recovered in the past will help us hold quality ownership investments during the down markets of the future.

Many individuals lost wealth by selling during down markets of the past 20 years. Great waves of selling generally occur during sharp market downturns. Critical to an investor's confidence during down times will be to understand who is managing the money, how long the manager has been producing positive results, and other considerations. I will begin to address these issues in the chapters that follow.

The Time to Buy

"The best thing about the future is that it only comes one day at a time."

Abraham Lincoln

Buy low and sell high. This is how investors make money, right? Endless advertisements on television for brokerage companies offer $9.95 or even less per trade. The message here is that we should all be traders, making economic forecasts and backing it up with savvy stock picks. There must be millions of "traders" out there fueling these brokerage firms. It can make investors feel like they are missing out if they don't use these brokerage companies.

We all have the experience of people telling a story of the great stock or mutual fund they bought and then tripled their money. Note that the stories of the losing trades and losing investments are much rarer. Even less common is the story of someone who has invested patiently for years, measuring results, and quietly refining methods and techniques over time.

The great challenge of trading is that one must be correct over a sequence of decisions. I don't think most people contemplate this when they hear that XYZ stock is the one to buy. The perennial optimism of the human condition goads us into thinking that we can buy at a great low price and then later sell at a profit. The reality is that if a stock goes down, an investor will get concerned and it will be difficult to buy more, even if the stock appears to be a bargain. When the stock goes up, we may either get excited and sell or hang on too long and see a slowing growth rate or decline.

Think of the lucky few who bought early into some great stock like Microsoft or, more recently, Google. After the doubling or tripling in value, what do you think happens? It is easy to think that a $10,000 initial investment grew to some huge multiple, but the reality for most of those lucky early investors is that the temptation to cash out was just too powerful. What about those who bought WorldCom or Level 3 Communications all the way down as $60, $40, and $20 became a great bargain for a stock that was surely going to $200 per share real soon? Take a look at the charts for these stock symbols (WCOM and LVLT) to see the rest of the story.

A huge industry exists in the selling of seminars, books, trading software, and all kinds of secret formulas to wealth. Advertisements say, "A few weeks of study are all it will take. Infinite riches await you when armed with our trading secrets." Where are the actual people who became wealthy doing this? I am confident there aren't many out there. Let's assume that if an individual creates a trading technique, system, or other structure that can be counted on for profits, he or she probably will not share it with anyone. The system will surely be exploited for maximum profits in extreme secrecy.

Professions in medicine and law are much less often promoted as something that can be learned by the layman. There are many reasons for this, but the greatest would be the huge barriers to entry. It is obvious to most that we cannot become our own physician or attorney, but if we just study enough we're sure we can pick the right companies to invest in. Getting rich by following some kind of secret formula or system is seductive and has been sold like bottles of snake oil throughout recorded history.

I am often appalled by the garbage concepts that I see being peddled on television. Charting of technical indicators and even currency trading is held out as something Mom can do from the kitchen table. AnyMom USA can get right in there, into that card game of infinite variables. She will be trading against teams of math savants in Chicago, Russian computer programmers, and endless forces dedicating their lives full time to the professional pursuit of profitable trades and asset management. Thus, the odds of success for most amateur traders are extremely low. Statistics on the success of trading at discount brokerage houses must be weak, or these firms would advertise their rates of success.

The idea of accumulating quality large-cap stocks for long-term investment is much different from the idea that you can consistently buy low and sell high. Selected leaders in multinational markets may be accumulated alongside a broadly diversified managed portfolio. I find this most often applies when investors have accumulated quality stocks—they do not necessarily need to be sold if one is willing and confident enough to hold long term. I do think that for most people, quality mutual funds are absolutely the best path. Once-storied companies like telecom companies and US auto manufacturers proved to be disastrous to their owners. These breakdowns in formerly reliable company stocks should alert us to the danger that concentration of an investor's portfolio in two or three blue chip stocks can prove to be disastrous.

Finding profitable entry and exit points over and over is very unlikely. Market timing is usually unsuccessful, yet many still confidently proclaim that they have a system that works. A simple solution to alleviate this problem is systematic investing, dollar cost averaging, value averaging, and other forms of regularly purchasing quality equity investments. If we can subscribe to the belief that the value of ownership rises over time, we can begin to ignore the day-to-day, quarter-to-quarter, and year-to-year fluctuations. This outlook is critical to the philosophy of long-term investors.

There are many historical examples of bewildering market declines that were simply temporary. It is easy to look back and see the obvious benefit of holding on until the inevitable recovery. It is much more difficult to live through down markets. The counterintuitive nature of investing does not lend itself to our natural psychological disposition as human beings. I have seen few with the courage to step up and buy at bargain prices during periods of fear and uncertainty. In general, we see the opposite. At the peak of the market in early 2000, we saw some of the greatest inflows into mutual funds ever. Conversely and, sad to note, the outflows (selling of mutual funds) were extremely high at the bottom near October 2002.

In the 1940s, there was a Cold War. In the late 1950s, Fidel Castro seized power in Cuba. President Kennedy was assassinated in the early

1960s in the decade that proceeded into the Vietnam War. Pick any time frame and look back, study the history, and realize that there will always be reasons to fear. This persistent uncertainty is what prohibits many from even considering becoming an owner.

I often contemplate the reasons behind the concentration of wealth. Why is it that some 80 percent of the wealth in this country (my estimate based on research) is controlled by 20 percent of the population? It is an insurmountable challenge for many of us to stomach the continuous ups and downs of ownership. Most simply do not have the persistence and stamina that ownership investing demands. The solution is understanding and trusting the holdings and management of one's portfolio. I spend much of my time as a professional advisor reminding and educating all kinds of investors of these historical truisms. To be confident when the market is difficult, we need to understand what we own, that our portfolio is broadly diversified, and that the shares in our portfolio represent quality companies with great future potential. Becoming an owner must be a lifelong pursuit, regardless of the mood of the market in any given year.

Holding on through difficult times is what success is made of. When an individual sets out on any challenging path, he or she is bound to encounter many disappointments and difficulties. Our American culture has forgotten this. This weakness of our spirit is preyed upon every day by financial companies selling products to the masses that have a theme of safety. The "safety" component of stability, of course, obscures the huge cost of low growth potential over time.

I am often dismayed when, after spending time and energy discussing these issues with a perfectly intelligent person, he or she asks, "So, what do you think the economy is going to do this year?" In many cases, I think that the person is not listening to me, and defaults to a question that seems to need to be asked. If you ask your advisor this question, you have missed my point. I feel that firms that put forth big economic forecasts for their clients are doing a huge disservice to them. Advisors who spend time discussing the economy are wasting your time.

There are numerous studies of the fallacious and unreliable nature of economic forecasting. It is often said that economists have predicted 10 out of the last 6 recessions. Most financial advisors have little formal economic education (which could be a good thing), but hopefully a good amount of investing knowledge. Specifically, if you are being guided by someone who spends a lot of time making predictions for the future, you may actually be in the presence of a fortune teller!

Financial predictions and forecasting become some sort of beauty pageant for financial firms. I always think of a noted economist who will remain unnamed … he had created a huge cottage industry for himself by predicting dire consequences associated with Y2K. He had an actual newsletter and website, and he made numerous television appearances speaking eloquently about the huge economic slowdown that was coming. There was endless discussion of the catastrophic consequences of a systemic computer programming flaw that was going to disrupt our entire economy at the stroke of midnight on December 31, 1999. What a wonderful story to sell to the people, playing on their fears! The idea was so simple to understand, and it made intuitive sense. But, it seems comical now—some garbage about the short-sighted computer programmers who neglected to accommodate years beyond 1999 in the base coding of many computer systems.

It is interesting to note that the year 2000 was also a huge year for religious zealots in the business of Armageddon predictions. Such a beautiful round number for our fears to attach themselves to! When it turned out to be just another New Year's Eve, the Armageddonists simply picked new calendar dates (the more crafty picked dates further out into the future) for their adjusted predictions. Many financial forecasters did the same.

Ironically, the gentleman behind the above Y2K global recession theory moved right on after being completely wrong and is still an active commentator on many a financial show. So many economists grind on and on, making predictions on top of forecasts without ever having a documented track record of what could have been earned or lost by following their advice.

The "dismal science" is a derogatory alternative name for economics devised by the Victorian historian Thomas Carlyle in the 19th century.

It is often stated that Carlyle gave economics the nickname "dismal science" as a response to the late 18th century writings of the Reverend Thomas Malthus, who grimly predicted that starvation would result as projected population growth exceeded the rate of increase in the food supply. If economics could be useful, you would think that governments would be able to avert more crises, but that is a pipe dream. Predicting the economic future is a dilemma akin to forecasting which card will be the next off a freshly shuffled deck of 52, only infinitely more difficult.

I staunchly believe that the more we try to predict even the near future, the more fearful we may become. A classic example of this is the fear mongering about the pending collapse of social security. Numerous high-level academic studies have shown that with structural adjustment, social security can last for many years. The real problem is with the health care costs in the senior population. Yet we hear the scary refrain of doom for social security over and over. The United States is an innovator in an increasingly modernizing global economy. The solution to our demographic problems will arise from innovations that no one can now predict.

So many huge variables are going to impact the actual experience of these programs that there is no point in prediction and certainly no benefit in worrying. Demographics, immigration, and macro economic cycles will determine the challenges we will face in the future. The most rational thing that an investor can do is to plan on a future. There is a future, and it will probably be served by quality businesses and organizations. As investors, we need a diversified portfolio of holdings of those companies.

The bear market of 2008 is a perfect example of how short-term thinking can lead to fear and irrational conclusions. There have been waves of pessimism based on very discouraging events that have unfolded since the fourth quarter of 2007. During these down markets, it begins to feel as if the market can never recover. The downturn in the global markets of 2008 has been driven by three primary trends:

- Reckless home mortgage lending and the subsequent credit or "sub-prime" crisis

- Global commodity price super spike

- Occupation of Iraq by US military

The long-term investor might say:

1.   Housing prices had previously appreciated at an unsustainable pace; the US will like continue to be a desirable place to own real estate, and the housing market will stabilize sooner rather than later.

2.   Many commodity bubbles succumb to supply/demand reality. Human innovation has always triumphed over shortage of a given natural resource. There are many near-future solutions to potential petroleum shortages, such as compressed natural gas, solar energy, and wind energy.

3.   Wars are the most tragic part of human history. Somehow, this too shall pass and the world will grind on.

The key to long-term investing success is to learn from the cycles of the past. The only way to "buy low" is to own through the down cycles with discipline and patience.

The Indexing Trap

"Things should be made as simple as possible, but not any simpler."

Albert Einstein

One of the most common pieces of advice in the financial media nowadays is the idea that the place to invest is inexpensive index mutual funds. "Just buy a low-cost total market index fund" and you will do great! There is much to be said for indexing and the savings in costs that it creates. Investors do, however, need to be cautious when considering blanket proclamations that indexing is always the answer.

It is important to understand what indexing actually is. The essential premise of indexing is to own a basket of stocks. Indexing is also referred to as "passive investing." We buy and hold a group of stocks or a "basket" of stocks that is grouped by a stock rating agency. The chosen stocks are selected by the rating agency. There is no money manager involved. There will be no qualitative judge to evaluate the stocks in a given index besides the rating agency that designs it.

Some of these baskets have been around for a long time. The most common is a basket of 500 well-known US companies. Indexing creates many distinct benefits to the investor. An important benefit of indexing is that it eliminates all the costs and trading of the money manager. The proponents of indexing would have you believe that the individuals managing your money are not adding any value, only cost. In many cases, I would agree with this given that what you pay for in your investments is money gone. Costs are a direct reduction of your end result. The question we must answer is whether there is a level of costs that creates value beyond the index.

The usual commentary suggests that the 500 Stock Index has outperformed 80 percent or 90 percent of all actively managed mutual funds. I find this to be generally true. I believe the reason for this is that a large number of publicly available mutual funds produce lackluster results. The reality is that equity money management is a monumentally difficult task that takes years of prudent, disciplined, and systematic work to produce meaningful results that might have some reasonable probability of persisting into the future.

As rational investors, we do not want to compare all mutual funds. We can limit our search to the largest 200 mutual funds publicly available. Why would we limit our search to the 200 largest funds? Because they create a group that has attracted the most money. It is rational to believe that the funds that attract the most money do so by producing quality results (I find this to be a very good way to screen for quality). The top 200 usually have a number of important criteria that we look for in money management. Characteristics such as a long track record, stable management, and ample resources are some of the most critical criteria we can look for in money management.

In my research using mutual fund data of the 10-year period ending June 30, 2007, out of the top 200 funds, many index funds did not perform in the top 100 versus US domestic stock funds. So why is it such common advice to use low-cost index funds as the recommended vehicle of choice? I believe it has to do with the self-serving nature of the media and media personalities who want to be advisors to the masses. The television personalities and book writers need you to believe that it will be easy to save thousands and even tens of thousands of dollars of costs over time by following their expert advice, reading a couple of books, subscribing to a newsletter, and placing your money in super low-cost index mutual funds or groups of index funds. Indexing is a great vehicle for those looking to dispense mass advice and broad rules of thumb.

I believe indexing breaks down even further when we look outside the US. It is much more difficult to create a list of 500 global stocks that we can count on to be consistently representative of the global economy. The variations in accounting standards, legal practices, and other critically important business issues that we face once we leave the US creates a much more complex proposition for global indexing.

But, it is essential to have quality global exposure in our long-term portfolios. Global indexes are areas that I believe create great difficulty in picking the baskets that comprise the index. Once you exit the US, the confidence factor in the index declines.

Indexing mutual fund companies have expanded the basket concept to many areas of investing. This dynamic creates many opportunities for disappointment. There are indexes for real estate, Japan, emerging markets, biotechnology, and on ad infinitum. Here, as in global indexing, the danger is that conditions will be less predictable than in the good old broad basket of 500 US blue chip stocks. Once again, the financial-industrial complex creates endless products and investment opportunities that exploit a particular concept. Whether or not that concept is actually producing results will only reveal itself over time. With a little research, you can see that the performance of many of these baskets and index vehicles does not hold out much benefit to the average portfolio.

I have often theorized that most of the people who advocate indexing as the smartest way to have money managed fall into two groups. The first group is book authors and other financial media personalities who want to convince the public that the only thing they need to do is follow the author's advice. I will say in many ways throughout this book … this is hogwash. So many life decisions and events will come along, such as buying a home, paying for college, and scary bear markets, that most do-it-yourselfers will never navigate these waters rationally without a personal advisor. All the costs that these investors may save by using index funds can be lost quickly through bad decisions made at critical moments.

The second group of indexing advocates is financial advisors who use index funds and now exchange-traded funds (ETFs) as baskets of stock to which they will then allocate. I am skeptical that the results of these types of portfolios are very good. The end result of this philosophy is to place the advisor in the role of money manager. I have seen so many advisory firms that have deluded themselves into thinking they have some sort of dynamic economic models that perform well. When you examine the poor track records of many of these firms, you often find lots of talk about managing risk and claims that "we take less risk than the market." This is often an excuse or explanation for underperformance.

This is not to say that certain index mutual funds cannot produce reliable, quality returns over time. I would simply treat index fund as any other money manager that needs to be monitored for quality results versus large institutional funds in its peer group. Note that I do not like comparing to all funds. I believe we can limit our pool of possible selection to the 200 largest funds available in each type or category that we choose to add to a portfolio. A constant problem we face as investors is the growing array of choices that are constantly available. It is an important and simple rule to only consider the large established money managers available.

Many large mutual funds use a systematic approach of some type in their management and stock picking. It is important to invest with a reasonable expectation that the historical results that we use to find quality mutual funds have a chance to be replicated in the future. The very largest funds are likely to be very systematic in their approach; with such huge pools of money, this is usually the case. There can never be any guarantee of future results, but the quality history of a mutual fund manager over a long period of 10 or even 20 years is a good screening criterion.

This discussion of the largest mutual funds leads us into another debate that I would like to make a brief comment on. A persistent criticism often voiced in the popular media, as well as in the financial planning trade, is often made against large money managers. The argument states that large funds can never be nimble enough to make timely trades that are profitable. If a fund has $20 billion or more to invest, it will be constrained by its sheer size. In most cases, this is probably true. There are, however, examples of small boutique, sophisticated trading shops that can produce outsized returns. In my research I have found that a lot of these funds have one of a number of problems. The list below reflects some of the problems I have found with small money managers:

- Small funds close when they a reach a certain asset size, becoming unavailable for investors to open new accounts.

- They invest in very volatile and unpredictable types of securities, creating a high level of volatility and making it difficult to hold on during the inevitable corrections and volatile markets.

- The managers that create the outperformance tend to want to go off on their own or change firms, cashing in on the celebrity of their outperformance.

- As a small fund creates high levels of performance, it will attract additional assets to change the nature of the fund. The performance may regress, or even deteriorate into a poor choice for the investors' money, as the asset size increases.

An argument can certainly be made that the effort to invest with small money managers can produce additional returns. But I believe that for most investors this pursuit will lead to lots of work and research. Ongoing monitoring and selection of small mutual funds become similar to the process of selecting individual stocks. If an investor pushes really hard, is really good, and has a high amount of luck, additional returns of 1 percent, 2 percent, or even 3 percent could be achieved. These additional returns will come with a higher level of risk, likely a higher level of cost, and a much higher workload for the investor. My anecdotal evidence of this would be that if you look at the list of top-performing mutual funds of the last one in five years, you will see that it is a constantly changing list. My theory here is that you will have to be very lucky, and very smart, to rotate to the group of funds that will be the best small funds for the next five years.

The indexing philosophy is driven primarily by the concept of driving down costs. Indexing also reduces the tendency of many money managers to falter in the face of challenging economic times or volatile markets. This is a concept that is definitely in indexing's favor. If we can drive out the human component, then those human emotions of greed, panic, and other defects will not present themselves.

This leads us to the question of who is designing the index. Shall we include the 500 largest companies in the world or just the US? Over the last 10 years, there has been a parade of "indexing" products that seek to refine the concept by introducing selection to the "index." This is simply a form of active investing, and indexing is no longer a passive investing concept.

Doing It Yourself

"The eye sees only what the mind is prepared to comprehend."

Henri Bergson

There has been a huge movement in the investment marketplace toward companies that assist investors in the task of managing their own money. These companies usually take the form of no-load mutual fund families or discount brokerage firms operating via the Internet. As we learn about all the cognitive deficits that we face as human decision makers, it bring us to the question of how these do-it-yourselfers perform with their investment portfolios.

People who have managed their own planning and investments often come into my office looking for validation that they do not need me or any other financial advisor. During the course of these conversations, I will usually ask, "What tools are this self-directed, non-professional money manager using to monitor performance? What sources of information is he or she using to make decisions?" I will then begin to explain that if you do not consistently compare your results to market averages, indexes, or elite mutual funds, you cannot know what your performance really is.

Notably, the discount brokerage firms do not seem to promote performance measurement. This is quite an amazing fact! There is readily available technology for the measurement and ongoing monitoring of a given portfolio's performance. These brokerage firms have made massive technology investments, but they seem to not emphasize tools that facilitate performance monitoring. Then again, why would firms that encourage trading be interested in measurement of the results? The notion that active trading by individual investors leads to positive results over time is questionable. I would consider it lunacy to think that any meaningful percentage of these traders can perform consistently over time. I have found that people have very selective memory when it comes to winning trades versus losers and stocks that stagnate.

The do-it-yourself myth applies to many things that people attempt in an effort to save costs or retain control. If you are going to redo your kitchen, you hopefully have been a professional carpenter recently. Portfolio allocation, asset management, and individual stock picking are both a very specialized profession and an artistic pursuit. It is an ever evolving challenge involving infinite variables. The variables include both internal company and market-specific characteristics of a given stock and external factors such as geopolitics. How will the end of a war or the decline of a currency affect a big Canadian company? What about the price of oil? Is there going to be a breakthrough with more energy-efficient automobiles? How will that affect Japanese and American manufacturers? The odds for most small investors who set out to trade stocks for profit are quite low in my opinion.

Think of the dilemma as a poker game, but without only 52 cards in the deck. This deck has a nearly infinite number of cards that can come up. The game will also be affected by weather patterns, political trends, and demographic phenomena.

We can all spend hours and hours reviewing financial statements, analyst reports, and government filings. If we work for a bank, we can become a financial-sector expert, and we can make savvy bank stock picks and become rich. If we work in the aerospace sector, we can make distinctions between the stocks in the aircraft business, military contracting, and other areas. I see this often with clients who hold the mistaken illusion that since they work in the industry, they can pick stocks in that industry. The idea here seems to be that people can simply open a discount brokerage account, pick their own stocks, and be their own money managers.

Recent market events would seem to support my position. Enron is a frequently cited example of how employees of a company felt misled and betrayed by the management of that company. There have been endless media stories, books, and movies studying the Enron fiasco. Litigation and endless investigations have yielded much information.

A number of high-level executives have been convicted, but many questions remain unanswered.

The lesson to take away from that horrific financial event begins with this question: How were people ruined by the collapse of one stock? Did those people ever see the old adage, don't put all your eggs in one basket? Did anyone point out that these people were happily skipping off to work every day with a basket full of all their eggs held in Enron stock? It is obvious that the do-it-yourself nature of the 401(k) era (with employer stock as an investment option) brought many to ruin.

Imagine that you worked at Enron in the late 1990s. Now picture yourself watching a rapid rise in the stock of a company where you worked. As the stock rose further and further, it would become increasingly difficult to resist. Employees would be talking about their 401(k) and how it became worth in excess of x thousands of dollars. Eventually, people who did not have all of their money in the stock would feel like they were missing out, or even that they were stupid.

The pressure would continue to build. People would begin to look beyond the assets of their 401(k) and open brokerage accounts and begin to borrow on margin. Visions of grand wealth, family legacies, and rich retirements would blind many investors to the mounting risk.

This story leads us to the sad interviews with many former Enron employees who lost all their retirement money. All the focus in this story has been on Enron management. "Management kept pumping the stock." "Our 401(k) was frozen and we couldn't make trades as the stock was going down." "We want our money back, and we are going to sue those who are responsible."

Why did they have all their money in Enron stock? That's the question we never hear! The reason many employees had all their money in Enron stock is that the stock was going up. The employees became greedy and overconfident in their abilities as investors. The employees were managing their investments themselves! Taking profits would only cut into the eventual pot of gold that all the newly minted geniuses could see in the future. Heck, everybody who worked there was going to make $10 million and then retire.

This process of small investors being run over and whipsawed by market manias has a long history. Years ago, it was common to hear "odd lot theory" mentioned as a tactical and strategic tool of professional investors. The concept here is that small purchases or odd lots (share transactions under 100 shares) are indicative of the smallest investor. Significant weight has been given to the idea that you could earn money by betting against what the little guy was doing. The recent mania of the late 1990s was a great example. The higher and more unreasonable prices became, the more interested the cab driver, brick layer, and dry cleaning proprietor became.

Many investors felt bewildered during this time. The nagging guilt of having "missed the boat" gnawed at investors on a daily basis. I readily admit to having been drawn into increasingly aggressive investments during this time, but I did have a great deal of skepticism that the market could continue its fast-paced assent. I look back on the model portfolios and allocations that I used during those heady years and they were far from perfect. I make no claim here as to my past performance as an investor. I did learn that the only way to employ your money is in long-term, broadly diversified portfolios.

When the crushing correction arrived at the beginning of March 2000, it was essential to be broadly diversified and hold firmly to the belief that values would recover in the long run. The notion that it was not good to sell into down markets, to continue to buy on a monthly basis, and to stay on plan was the only way to hang on during one of the most damaging market corrections in modern history. By staying true to fundamental asset allocation strategies, most long-term portfolios have gone on to recover from the bear market of 2000 to 2002.

One huge drawback to trading for yourself is what I call the "vacuum effect." Once you begin to manage money for yourself, you will be by yourself. Over time, you will not form a relationship with an advisor or groups of advisors with whom you have built a foundation of trust. Decisions will need to be made alone, without the benefit of seeing numerous others in your peer group, the dilemmas they face, and what all the options might be.

No-load mutual fund investing is a much different proposition from trading individual stocks. The odds of success for the do-it-yourself investor are greatly improved through the resource of low-cost, professional money management. There has been a massive proliferation of direct-to-consumer mutual fund offerings. Larger no-load firms offer in excess of 200 of their own funds, and they offer access to hundreds more from other fund firms. Many of these firms are constantly introducing new funds, sector funds, exchange-traded funds (ETFs), and other untested ideas that could create confusion and poor results for all but the most sophisticated and persistent people who choose to go it alone.

Building a relationship with an ethical, competent professional advisor takes a long time. At what point do the people managing their own money begin to turn over some of their asset management to trusted professionals? As people get older, and the need for guidance becomes more obvious, how will that relationship be formed? I do not think many do-it-yourself investors have a strategy for building advisory relationships in addition to their own individual money management. This comes from healthy skepticism about financial people. "Who can ever care more about my money than me?" This natural distrust has been earned over many years of questionable events and practices perpetrated by the financial-industrial complex.

Combine this natural cynicism of the public investor with the fact that many of the financial products in the marketplace work on the very principle that the worse the product the agent or marketing company sells to you, the more he or she will be paid. This is a dynamic that I have rarely seen written about. We all need to understand that given equal compensation, a financial marketing firm or salesperson will select the best program for a given client. The reality of the marketplace is that there is a wide range of compensation rates among different investment products. The most blatant example I have found is in the area of state-regulated insurance products. I believe state regulation is overburdened and subject to finesse and manipulation of insurance companies seeking approval for heavily loaded annuities and cash value life insurance policies that are sold to people as investments.

The fact of the matter is that the general public has an intelligence that is perfectly perceptive to the years of manipulation and opaque financial products that have been sold. No-load and other self-directed investment opportunities and mutual fund companies grew out of this environment to become some of the largest financial service companies in the marketplace. Much of this has resulted in healthy competition, benefiting the consumer. With today's powerful Internet-based technologies, and software-based allocation and management tools, self-management seems like a no-brainer.

The environment of financial product marketing has driven many investors to distrust financial advisors. I use the term advisor quite loosely here. Many financial product-marketing institutions refer to their salespeople as consultants, advisors, and other terms that tend to mask the pure salesperson/prospect relationship that exists. It cannot be stressed enough here, the commission-based distribution system drives the worst investment products to offer the greatest compensation to marketers and salespeople. Programs with high fees, long penalty periods, and other negative qualities simply must pay more to get distributed.

I run into this time after time in the process of meeting with new clients. The most striking example that I find is that of an insurance company that offers the same product with low, medium, and high cost structures available. The only difference is that the highest cost structure will be the most lucrative to the insurance company (and the selling agent). Often, financial product companies try to mask this obvious conflict of interest with minor technical or cosmetic differences in the product. In a great percentage of these cases, I find that the "advisor" has chosen the highest-cost plan. The cost differences are usually never discussed, and the consumer's experience is one of deception, bait and switch, and financial product companies charging the absolute highest price that the market will bear, with the legal minimum disclosure of actual costs.

This lack of concern for the consumer's best interests creates a reputation that has been earned over long periods of time by Wall Street, insurance companies, and many types of financial product marketing institutions. From Wall Street firms to small regional insurance companies, the exploitation of the consumer was a practice that persisted for many years. Prior to May 1, 1975, stock brokerage commissions were fixed and there was no price competition for trading in individual securities on the New York Stock Exchange. After May 1, 1975, fixed commissions were abolished. A massive opportunity was created for discount brokerages, direct marketing, and no-load mutual fund companies to compete on quality and low cost. The feeling of dealing directly with the mutual fund company was vastly superior to the experience that many investors had in their dealings with major Wall Street firms.

As this competition grew, people had many options and the allure of making their own decisions enticed many to abandon the idea that having an advisor had any value whatsoever. The law of unintended consequences has now produced an environment where these no-load companies have proliferated to such a degree that I believe they are now the source of much confusion and disappointment for those who attempt to go it alone.

This proliferation of options for investor self-reliance has re-created many of the same dynamics that existed before the competition arrived in 1975. No-load firms must expend massive sums on branding and mass marketing. Proven, low-cost mutual funds are not the attention-grabbing products that will allow the financial-industrial complex to grow ever more wealthy and powerful. It is the program that has gimmicks and shiny, optimistic projections that gather the marketing mojo. The healthy, long-term guidance that most investors need is lost in a sea of glitz and marketing.

The pendulum has swung far from the golden age of fixed Wall Street commissions and restrained competition (hitting many people right in the head!). Financial companies marketing directly to the public have become massive forces in the marketplace. These gigantic asset-gathering companies have come a long way since the days when most mutual funds charged a load of 8.5 percent. The direct-to-the-public financial product companies came into a marketplace in the 1970s that was ripe for price competition. Many of the high-cost products of the pre-no-load age have been driven from the market.

Unfortunately, this competition has led to a proliferation of firms and products vying for a share of investors' precious assets. The sheer mass of advertising that I witness every day from these no-load and discount brokerage companies has a monumental cost that must be recovered through higher costs and fees.

The endless pharmaceutical marketing is another market distortion similar to this. Now that drug companies are competing on television and other forms of media, we all pay higher prices for our drugs. I also cite the analogy of airline deregulation as another example of how this process of competition after an era of regulation can lead to huge un-intended costs and downside for the consumer. Competition in the air travel business created large cost savings and other consumer benefits in its early days. But, the endless cost-cutting has made air travel quite a perilous proposition, with passengers treated like cattle being herded on to planes.

As of this writing, I personally much prefer the old-fashioned road trip. Air travel satisfaction seems to have been on a continuous decline for as long as I can remember. Take a look at air safety statistics, and other measures, and I do not think it is a stretch to conclude that cost-cutting can lead to unforeseen problems. Discount air travel has led to cuts in safety and other areas that are frightening to ponder. Maybe it should be a little more expensive to fly if we want it to continue to be a pleasurable way to travel. This safety and satisfaction measure should also apply to one's financial journey.

The costs of financial services to consumers have been cut greatly in the era of deregulation. Now that costs have been squeezed to such a low level, you are left with a playing field filled with competitors that must create novelty and marketing campaigns to capture investor as-sets. Unfortunately, novelty and marketing will be unlikely to produce the result that we would hope for as a society.

The two largest no-load mutual fund companies now offer more than 450 mutual funds between them. I continually wonder how an individual can optimize his or her own portfolio on an ongoing basis. A recent advertising campaign, running in heavy rotation on television, talks about "free objective advice." An auto insurance company has been advertising for a number of years that it will compare the rate it offers to that of other companies. How is this possible? Do these companies need to recoup the huge cost of television advertising through the fees that their own products generate? Of course, these costs will be charged to the end user or those companies will cease to exist.

A glaring example of marketing without regard to the benefit to the customer is a campaign I have noticed recently by discount brokerage firms advertising tools to "back-test" your investment strategy. The message here is that smart do-it-yourselfers out there are coming up with investment concepts that can then be back-tested against history. Then, you can take your proven formula and place your winning trades. They fail to mention that back-testing has little proof as a valid tool for investment selection. These are huge network and major cable channel dollars going into something that will lead people to the false impression that back-testing is something that can actually work.

While on the subject of historical testing of a specific strategy, just think about the last three decades. The great investment strategies of the 1970s were much different than those of the 1980s and 1990s and so on. It is my opinion that anyone who talks about back-testing should be avoided. Why would such a concept be advertised and promoted with the massive cost of television advertising? This is just another example of marketing the sizzle, not the steak. These discount brokerage firms are promoting a tool that can be compelling to an individual investor looking for that magic formula to wealth. Back-testing has become cheap to offer due to the decline in the costs of computing power and the ease of delivery by Internet to the end user. I remain highly skeptical that a tool of this type could yield any consistent results for users who may be drawn in without knowing that there is no proof of historical back-testing being effective.

There are endless examples in the marketplace today evidencing the fact that we have come full circle from the days of fixed commissions.

The cost reduction offerings of the no-load product companies have now become a force in the marketplace that must compete on something other than price. The good part is that costs have been reduced, and transparency has risen. The challenge is that, with competition and proliferation of choice, the lone wolf faces an overwhelming amount of data to analyze from thousands of products in the marketplace. It is in this complex investment world that the trusted, independent advisor becomes invaluable.

In most cases, an individual investor managing his or her entire portfolio will experience periods of great uncertainty. All of the investing community constantly faces an endless string of that infinite list of variables. Over mid- and long-term periods, the vacuum will become more and more isolating. We can also imagine that as investors get into their sixth and seventh decade of life, the complications of aging create serious risks. As the investment portfolio becomes all the more critical to address rising income needs in health care and other general assistance, are Bob and Betsy going to begin interviewing for the position of trusted advisor? If Bob and Betsy go into the hospital, who will make their decisions if they cannot?

This is a dynamic characteristic I might call the widow/widower shock. Usually in a do-it-yourself household, I find that one or the other spouse is the "money person." I often wonder who will be there to be trusted and make tough decisions if something happens to that money person. One of the greatest drawbacks to this do-it-yourself concept is the frequent lack of a backup plan. There is no one more vulnerable to the dark side of the financial marketplace than someone recently widowed or divorced.

When managing one's own money, there is the additional risk of lack of objectivity. We will continue to resist admitting errors much longer with our own money than a true professional will. The skilled advisor will dispassionately rebalance your portfolio. The trusted guide will ruthlessly eliminate mutual funds and asset managers when they fail to meet peer group and other measurement criteria.

I think that removing subjective emotions from the process of managing one's own account can add up to better long-term average returns. I have spoken with an endless list of sophisticated people who are quick to tell me of current doubts about the market or outlook for future gains. Many self-directed investors I have seen often seem fixated on the level of the market or the idea that they can actually pick individual stocks that will produce results over time. My mind always begins to question the wisdom of amateur economic forecasting and stock picking.

Obviously, as a professional advisor myself, my bias is toward that of working with an advisor. This is not to say that I think being active in the process of your investment decisions is a bad thing. Some of the most productive portfolios that I have had the good fortune to work with have belonged to those individuals who actively participate with me in ongoing monitoring and selection of a given investment portfolio. We must always remember that a positive advisor-client relationship takes many years to build and should be one of informed partnership between the advisor and the investor.

Thirty Seconds and a Web Site

"There is nothing so useless as doing efficiently that which should not be done at all."

Peter F. Drucker

The modern financial product firm seems focused primarily on mass marketing. The huge amounts of advertising dollars spent on television, naming rights of stadiums, and sponsorships of athletes and golf tournaments are an accepted reality of the financial-industrial complex. There is nothing wrong with advertising as a way to build brand awareness and market many types of products and services. But, financial products and services are abstract and different and may not be communicated very well in 30-second sound bites or long-term brand awareness campaigns.

When an automobile company incurs advertising expenses, they will have to be mitigated by increased sales or reduced profits. The competitive market price of the vehicle will determine the actual volume of sales. With financial products, the dynamics are much different. The costs of advertising can be built into the asset charge of the product where the consumer may not be aware of it without the required knowledge and attention to detail. The fee structure of the investment may rise in the future. The mutual fund company may cut back on research or other costs to increase future profits at the expense of account holders. There are many ways that the costs of marketing can erode the value of the financial product without this cost being easily understood by the consumer.

The costs of mass marketing financial products are just the beginning. After the massive advertising dollars have been spent, the modern solution will be to drive costs down through technology. The World Wide Web has brought about an absolute paradigm shift in the reach of financial product marketing. Your advisor can now be a web login. There seems to be this growing notion that all you need to make financial decisions is a brand name that you recognize and a web portal. The investor can then choose from gigantic menus of choices or allocated portfolios, such as conservative, moderate, or aggressive, that are set up by the financial company.

The Internet is an incredible resource that is continually evolving. Once an investor has chosen which provider to place assets with, a number of problems can develop. The financial firm now has a client who will only shop at that firm's supermarket. I think consumers feel a false sense of security with a firm that will conduct business directly, without the greedy sales rep to badger them. There seems to be a great danger in the isolation that people tend to experience when interacting through a computer-based interface.

I do not think that the large Internet-based firms are relentlessly looking for ways to create better returns for their clients. Rather, they work toward the profitability of the firm first. Another problem that I see here is that of the cookie-cutter solution. We are so unique and have such different lives and goals. Some are looking to travel and spend. Some want to leave the maximum inheritance for their children. There are many nuances in the course of a lifetime of financial decisions. Our modern existence is an endless string of these personal, monetary decisions. These decision sequences are difficult to address through mass-marketed software-based solutions.

If Bob purchases the wrong car, he may be unhappy for three to five years. If Bob makes a sequence of poor or irrational financial decisions, his future may be permanently damaged. This is why we have school counselors starting in elementary all the way through to graduate school. Education, like financial management, is a process, not a momentary decision. We need to continually refine and reassess what we can do to become stronger.

The passive model of the Internet is likely to breed periods of interest, followed by gaps in oversight and evaluation. If I do not enter data expressing the changes in my situation, is the web site going to ask me?

Programmers and web consultants will argue that we can set endless reminders and program for all of these watershed moments in life. I am not so sure. Programmers have had difficulty in creating a computer that can play better bridge than the best human champions can due to probabilistic factors. Bridge is certainly a complex game, but it does not compare to the complexity that we face through decades of life and the planning and decision making that go along with it.

There is another dynamic here in the notion that we can serve the masses in a low-cost, centralized way. Top-down decision making has very poor application in helping people make important financial decisions on their own. I do not believe for one minute that groups of intelligent consultants can create a platform that will help people stay current and make rational decisions. I witness examples regularly when individuals come into my office with questions regarding basic issues of their 401(k). I find that the Internet portal interface that many 401(k) plans offer can cause utter confusion for many plan participants.

As discussed previously, indexing is a popular mechanism even in light of the fact that many elite mutual funds have provided greater returns. This mass market solution fits in very nicely with indexing. We can go ahead and toss our money into a series of index strategies along with our Internet servicing platform.

As an advisor, I am perplexed by the fact that under the 401(k) retirement model in this country; it is difficult for me to counsel and advise clients on the issue of retirement. In most retirement and 401(k) plans, no mechanism provides the ongoing data and balance information to an advisor. There is very little for most advisors to do if we cannot get paid for monitoring and advising our clients regarding their largest asset.

The reality of this issue is that most people will not take an active role in their investment decisions until they are much older. Pushing people to save at the highest possible rate and allocate to equities with the goal of long-term wealth creation is a process that is difficult to automate. Mass marketing and cookie-cutter approaches for the middle and upper-middle class of the US is not the solution to greater financial strength and intelligence. These dynamics are as likely to help the average individual become richer as mass pharmaceutical advertising is to help people become healthier.

Healthy Relationships

"Consider the following. We humans are social beings. We come into the world as the result of other's actions. We survive here in dependence on others. Whether we like it or not, there is hardly a moment of our lives when we do not benefit from other's activities. For this reason it is hardly surprising that most of our happiness arises in the context of our relationships with others."

The Dalai Lama

Healthy relationships in life are one of the greatest goals that we can hope to achieve. This discussion of the downside of do-it-yourself investing leads me to thoughts of the ideal financial advisor relationship. This relationship or set of trusted advisors will determine what level of success can be achieved.

These bonds of trust are not built overnight. Love at first sight can be a very dangerous thing when it comes to trusting an advisor to handle your money. An easily recognized warning sign for the consumer of advice is pressure and urgency to make transactions or move money from existing investments.

When an "advisor" wants to move all your accounts right away or make big changes as an opening part of your engagement with him or her, watch out. So often I will see some poor soul pressured into moving all assets to some type of account or plan that has no obvious benefit, or even worse. There is usually some sales tactic or urgency created by the marketer or salesperson. I always remember my father helping me slow down and reminding me that "they will still be building them tomorrow" in the buying decision of various types of things. This advice is critical when making financial decisions that can have a drastic impact for many years.

A teaser interest rate, bonuses, or limited/urgent offerings are a great warning to continue your search for an advisor. Very often, there is a great urgency to "close" the sale, although the consumer is not really aware of being sold. I have seen many cases where investors felt that there was urgency to move all of their retirement money to a new investment. Often, I have witnessed high-pressure tactics stressing a "bonus" interest rate or other limited-time opportunity that motivates the exploited to sign.

Very large emotional components for investors' decisions revolve around fear. I have witnessed marketers of financial products targeting this fear relentlessly. Professionally competent advisors know that investment results take time, diversification, and cooperative markets. Fear is now. We can start today to protect against the disaster du jour! Watch for the quick approach of sales reps telling you to be afraid, be very afraid and we can protect you!

This fear mongering has been going on for a very long time. Any message from a financial professional that stresses the fear emotion is a great warning sign of a defect in that advisor or sales rep. This is often difficult for the average investor to detect. "Jim is so concerned that I might lose money." "Sally is not a greedy broker who will put me at risk." These types of messages are very comforting.

The appeal to fear is a sure sign of an agenda that may not be in the investor's best interests. The human emotional spectrum is greatly biased toward fear. Financial product marketing companies are acutely aware of this. The appeal of a "safe" investment can be as much as three times more appealing to our subconscious as that of a potential for gain. Anxiety and uncertainty is a constant that needs to be tolerated in the short run, and if a prospective advisor plays to these issues, that is a reason to keep searching for someone who can help you see the long-run potential and risks in a balanced and rational way.

Another pitfall for one who seeks a competent advisor is what is known as "the expert service problem." If you want to have a plumbing problem resolved or your car fixed, what are you going to do? You will get the diagnosis and the treatment from the same individual. This is fine if you have a sinus infection and you visit your doctor, but you will look for a second opinion when you need heart surgery.

The difficulty is that you will trust the same source for the diagnosis and treatment of your need. There is no easy answer to this issue. The full disclosure of all costs and fees is a starting point. An advisor who has a strong, clear commitment to open communication and consistency is critical.

Fiduciary responsibility that the advisor takes on is critical to the investor. The fiduciary duty is a legal relationship between two or more parties. A fiduciary duty is the highest standard of care imposed at either equity or law. A fiduciary is expected to be extremely loyal to the person to whom the fiduciary owes the duty (the client). Fiduciaries must not put their personal interests before this duty, and must not profit from their position as a fiduciary, unless the client consents. This is currently an area undergoing great debate and discussion in the financial industry.

Many investors are surprised to learn that various types of insurance and securities licensing do not mandate the fiduciary level of ethics for representatives serving the public. It would seem quite obvious that many of the lousy financial products, mutual funds, and insurance contracts that are targeted to consumers could not be marketed by individuals who adhere to the strict standards of fiduciary responsibility. It is also important to point out that no code of professional standards can prevent unethical practices. I strongly believe that having a candid discussion about advisors' ethical standards of practice is one of the first things that the investor needs to do.

Transparency and clear cost disclosure is critical to a positive advisor/client relationship. In some cases, it may make sense to pay a commission and at other times a fee is the right way to go. The core issue here is an easily understood cost structure that is explained in an understandable and straightforward way.

The nature of the expert/service relationship is something that will reveal its quality slowly as the investment has a chance to grow. It is important to listen for consistency in what your advisor says. Often I see investment professionals turn on a dime in terms of what they have advised in the past. Changing market conditions are an easy justification for an endless stream of changes in strategy and portfolio structures. Watch for consistency as an important sign of trustworthiness.

Performance measurement is another critical area that I see as confusing for all of us, professionals and investors included. We need to consistently measure our results against the general market and peer groups of similar investments. Endless games are played here by advisors and financial firms. I have seen many ridiculous performance reports using positive comparisons that are completely contrived. The reality here is that no portfolio or advisor is going to be perfect all the time. We need to approach Mr. Market and the process of investing with great humility and an ability to periodically concede mistakes. The danger here that I often see is that these "confessions" are used as justification to change a portfolio and try something new.

I also see many financial advisors under the illusion that they must know the answer to any and all questions asked. Social security, car insurance, student loans, and grants … there are endless issues that no one person will have all the answers to. Sometimes the best answer is "I do not know, but I will try to help you find accurate information." Be wary of the overconfident and all-knowing experts. A process of thinking through the issues that confront us in a rational and systematic way is what great advisors are able to deliver. Investing is a humbling process in which even the great businesspeople and money managers frequently are proven wrong or foolish. This is particularly true in the short term. Arrogant attitudes are a sure sign of the pride that comes before the fall.

Another pitfall that I have seen with great frequency is what I call the "referral of trust." This happens with someone's brother's advisor, co-worker, best friend, long-time neighbor, or some such relationship. People go in with the notion that "this guy made great money for my brother." They enter the relationship with the guard dog of healthy skepticism at the kennel.

There are two great problems in this situation. First, it is ripe for abuse. Investors come in with their defenses down, and the advisor charges what the traffic will bear. The cousin or sister or whoever that has been referred is coming to the advisor already convinced of quality, even though he or she may have never really understood how to measure results versus the proper peer group. The only thing that may have been good about a particular advisor is that the market happened to be going up.

These are critical issues that people never even think of. It is the problem of the blind leading the ignorant. As harsh as this may sound, when I hear that this advisor did great for so-and-so, my first question is, compared to what? Often, the investors will have no idea that they should have significantly more gains in the account! The advisor certainly is not going to bring it up. People are often satisfied if the account has not lost money. The powerful psychological bias against losing money is a huge factor in many cases that I witness where people have thought they were doing well simply by not losing.

Often, the perception of results and actual quality money management and advice do not go hand in hand. People love to love their advisor. They want to believe that their advisor is smart, exclusive, and a good reflection on them. In many instances, investors simply do not want to hear the facts of how they are being led down a questionable road. Often, I am simply looked upon as a competitor who is after money. Even in cases where I advise a second opinion other than mine, people often refuse to listen to criticism or even make the effort to get further information.

Obviously, bad experiences with advisors result in very little in the way of referrals, but I think this is often a function of the direction of the market. The fact is that when people see growth, they often conclude that their account and advisor are "good." I have seen cases where an account has been paying below market interest or charging high fees for 10 or even 15 years, and still the holder is not angry when confronted with these facts. This often happens when someone has the misfortune of working with a captive agent of an insurance company. The investor has been fed costly insurance-based investments for years. A competent advisor comes in, presents the sad reality, and is met with great disdain and skepticism.

People are often closed minded and adversarial toward constructive criticism about their advisor. Being informed that you have been misled in something that you have not fully understood from the beginning is frightening.

I learned about this in a powerful way when I entered the profession. Retirement annuities had been sold to people who paid very high commissions. The marketing was very easy, because the annuity had a higher stated rate of interest than almost any of the competitors. The catch was that the annuities were known as two-tier annuities. The concept was that you could see a higher rate of interest, but that rate only applied to an "annuity value." That value was only available if you took an annuitized payout from the insurance company where it had great leverage in the payout phase. Thus, the higher rate of interest was an illusion, because the insurance company could control the interest rate during the payout phase. Worse yet, if you wanted your money more quickly, say for better market-based opportunities, you would get a separate value called a surrender value. The differential between the "annuity" and "surrender" value would start high, say 10 percent or 20 percent (representing the commission that had been paid) and then the disparity between the two values would grow larger because the insurance company was paying a lower rate of interest on the surrender or actual cash value.

Needless to say, these were not very good financial products and subsequently there was significant litigation against the creators and sellers of these types of products. Many times when I sat in meetings where the facts were presented to account holders, the victims of the lousy investments felt insulted by the facts! They did not want to believe that they were part of a bad decision. In many cases, the account holders really liked their advisor and referred him or her to friends and family. "My advisor is a great guy; he would never hurt me on purpose." Yeah, I'm sure he had no idea!

I came to understand that the marketers who were selling these costly, restrictive annuities actually believed that they were doing a good thing. The high rates of commission have a way of co-opting the sales reps into being great believers in the merits of a particular product. I saw situations where the "advisor" would come to clients who were closing their account and vehemently defend the product and pressure the investor. As people became aware of class action litigation years later, they were more amenable to accepting the negative characteristics of these plans.

The simple solution for many of these consumers would have been to ask, "What is your compensation if I choose to invest in this recommendation?" The answer in the case of a high-commission financial product should provide some clarity as to the integrity of a given advisor. A classic answer is "the company pays the cost." This is a misleading, if not flat-out fraudulent, statement. There is always a cost to the investor when money is placed into any kind of packaged product. The costs are generally equal to the effort made to push the product. The higher the energy placed into the sales pitch, the higher the costs usually are.

We must remember here that there is no Hippocratic oath in the field of financial product sales. There has been a great increase in the discussion of sales practices and standards of conduct, and I believe this is an encouraging development. The impact of all these efforts by regulators and financial companies on the quality of what the consumer ends up with is very much an open question. You do not hear any talk of the insurance, mutual fund, or mortgage industry implementing a pledge to first do no harm. What I do see happening is that the companies are making efforts to protect themselves from future litigation, while creating products that are more and more complex and opaque.

In consultations with those who have been sold costly, underperforming, or just plain lousy financial products, I find a huge humiliation factor. Often, telling people that they have made poor investments is like telling them that they are bad parents. Rather than look at the process and advisor that led to the lackluster results, people tend to make excuses. They talk about how "I don't gamble" and "I lost a lot of money before I got into this plan."

There is powerful loyalty and inertia that comes with investing. This becomes detrimental when the investor has been led to costly, complex, or overly conservative strategies or products. A common situation that

I witness repeatedly is an investor saying, "I asked my advisor for the real safe choice." What happens in this all too common situation is that fear and outright scare tactics are often used. The consumer ends up requesting the "safe" fixed investment after having been scared witless. A powerful additional factor here is that the easiest investment to service is one that never fluctuates. Fixed annuities are a great example of this. They can provide high compensation for the sales rep and great "safety" to the investor. The reality is that many fixed annuities are so costly that the investor would end up with greater appreciation in a bank money market account.

A competent advisor will constantly look to refine and improve rather than defend, explain, or justify. Often, the sign will be that the advisor will self-criticize and seek to work hard to explain with information that can be readily understood. If a portfolio has started out on a sound, long-term performing platform, these adjustments should be easy to make, with little or no added costs.

There is deep psychological fear for many people when it comes to investments and financial products. There is good reason for this. When we eat a good-quality meal, drive a well-manufactured automobile, or shop at a quality retailer, it is easy to evaluate and have reasonable confidence in the value received. Investing is a completely different proposition. The highest quality advisors and money managers will often have down years. The process of creating quality results can take three or even five years to begin to emerge.

A good indicator of quality and trustworthiness is for the advisor to continually compare to the peer groups of the mutual fund or money managers that comprise the portfolio. Consistent, easily understood, and straightforward reporting of account performance is an important sign of a competent advisor.

Churches, health clubs, golfing buddies, and other social situations help all of us to form networks that can assist in seeking important relationships. The same environments have produced Ponzi schemes and many horrible financial frauds. I am not saying that these situations are always bad, but I often see that people don't measure properly or get out and compare. Sadly, it is my belief that religious connections are breeding grounds for questionable product marketing. This mischief is brewed from the implied trust of the house of worship, whatever denomination it may be. Be wary of people who come to a religious environment to discuss money. What they are often there to do is market expensive financial products that yield high commissions.

The process of financial trust and guidance is one that grows like a tree. It is a long, slow process. I frequently have seen someone who has four, five, or even six different individual retirement accounts (IRAs). Their advisor was simply pulling off the shelf something different every year. Sure, sometime there are reasons to make changes, but generally good money management will repeat. It can be built on over time. Inconsistency is a warning sign. If you're offered some new idea every two or three years, go interview some other advisors.

Big financial companies are often guilty of this inconsistent pattern. I think it is something that they use to their advantage. Every few years or so, some hot new firm will be doing great things. This is good for the financial product company, but not at all good for the investor who gets in after the short-term streak of high results. The track record is always starting over with some new concept. The uninformed investor perceives this as the advisor doing his or her job, but in reality the investor is never staying long enough for the fund manager to work through a full cycle. Now, of course, many people are making good consistent returns for their clients. But I do believe many are constantly producing the financial sausage, and it is not good for your portfolio's health. Continually chasing the latest hot mutual fund or manager can be very costly over time.

Another misperception is that many people view mutual funds and investing in general as a commoditized process. Investors should treat the selection of an advisor the same way they would treat the choice of a heart surgeon. Turning over trust and money to another person is one of the most important decisions that we can ever make. It is as far from a commoditized process as there is. As discussed in many different ways in this book, investing and money management is a mixture of art and science. The differentials between the mediocre and elite can mean the difference between the beauty of financial strength and bitter insecurity.

The common perception that many people feel toward their investments or advisor can be a detrimental characteristic. It is healthy to have an ongoing evaluation of the performance of portfolio strategies of a given firm or advisor. High-quality advisors will use an ever evolving set of tools to report performance versus various peer groups and indexes.

This is an important quality to watch for in your advisor relationship—the ability of your advisor to self-criticize and take responsibility when things do not turn out as hoped. Obviously, these comparisons can be subjective and it is an ethical challenge to an advisor to fess up to periodic underperformance. From time to time, all strategies will underperform. This is to be expected and discussed in a rational and healthy way be any good advisor.

The buck starts and ends with your trusted advisor. Even when the shortcoming may be someone else's mistake, I always try to say that I should not have let the situation occur. I find that when I step up and take responsibility for a mistake or disappointment, we all feel better and can move on. Someone who has the ability to say, "I am sorry," "I should not have let this happen," or "I take full responsibility" is probably worthy of trust.

The discipline, patience, and long-term commitment required for creating financial strength gives birth to a psychological loyalty to our investments. When we begin to see the mid- and long-term results of ownership of quality companies that our portfolio contains, a confident loyalty can begin to grow. Together with a competent advisor, the investor/owner can benefit from a continuously growing belief that whatever scares, manias, or panics we face, the value of ownership will create a foundation for growing financial strength.

I see this growing sense of calm and loyalty in my everyday interactions with clients. The longer they have held a given investment that has produced quality results, the less those investors will concern themselves with periods of decline or market turmoil. The process is analogous to the process of education … we have graduated when we can be confident in our belief that ownership works.

The Car Salesman, The Supermarket, or The Architect

"Every man takes the limits of his own field of vision for the limits of the world."

Arthur Schopenhauer

Where are you when you get your information and advice? Not many people think of it in these terms, but the process of investing can be greatly affected by the underlying structure of the environment you have entered. When you walk into a car dealership, are the sales reps going to help you make objective comparisons between different manufacturers' products? Not very likely! The bias is a given. Comparisons will not be made in an objective way and we should know this as we walk in the front door. The clerks and salespeople are there to move that manufacturer's inventory as quickly as possible at the highest price possible. They are trained to keep you there and not let you leave until you have purchased today's great bargain.

This is the situation that occurs when a financial product company employs its own employees as "advisors" or "financial consultants." Many of the largest name brands in the financial world are structured this way. The financial mega firms are living examples of the financial-industrial complex in action. These financial behemoths are involved at every level of the financial product food chain. Their activities include investment banking, trading, mutual fund creation and management, and, of course, financial advice for individuals, businesses, and 401(k) plans. I have observed the proprietary product bias of these firms for years. Great efforts are made by these companies to obscure this reality. A client of this type of financial firm will often be told that "we handle all the different products in the marketplace with objectivity." Upon examination of the portfolio, however, we find a high proportion of those companies' proprietary products or programs.

Insurance companies and banks have made huge inroads into almost all areas of financial services. The barriers that once were in place to protect consumers from conflicts of interest have been razed through the heavy political lobbing efforts of these massive forces in the consumer marketplace. It remains to be seen what the consequences will be to the unleashing of the banks to sell depositors market-based financial products, insurance, and investments. It is my strong belief that banks have a conflict of interest here and should not be allowed into the investment marketplace. Remember, when you walk into good old First National, you have just stepped into a dealership for all the proprietary bank and non-bank products that the bank wants to sell. The recent consumer mortgage market fiasco is a strong indication of the absence of any notion of fiduciary responsibility inside the banking industry.

The banks have, in my opinion, a huge quality deficit when it comes to areas outside the core business of banking. There is a simple reason for this that stems from the banking culture and attitude that the banks have about the relationship of the bank and depositor. The marketing and capital investment in offices and branch bank locations is a powerful marketing and relationship-building tool. The banking institutions seem to have a sense that they own the customer.

When banks enter the market for financial services and invest-ment advice, ideally they would produce a culture that promotes a customer-centric environment that can be a resource for investment education and guidance. This simply does not happen in reality. It would be the same as asking a Ford dealer to educate its loyal customers about all the different brands of vehicles on the market, and if that customer chose a non-Ford vehicle, a small sales fee would be paid to the dealer.

There is growing sentiment among market commentators that the repeal of the Glass-Steagall and Banking Act of 1935 has created the environment that greatly contributed to the housing crisis that is now unfolding. These Depression-era laws were enacted to prohibit large private banks whose chief business was investment banking from receiving deposits. These laws that mandated the separation of risk-based banking from deposit-based banking were repealed at the very end of the Clinton era in 1999. The Gramm-Leach-Bliley Act of 1999 has formalized this free-for-all environment in which large financial conglomerates operate.

Investors need to understand that this is a whole new world and protect themselves accordingly. The mortgage debacle is a strong signal of the dangers created by the breaking down of laws that existed for more than 50 years. This housing meltdown is symbolic of the financial ignorance of the masses in the United States. My father used to say that when he was a kid, people who drove a Cadillac really had wealth. There were no dealers advertising "no credit, no problem" and enticing people into purchases that they could not afford. In the culture of instant credit, anyone can own just about anything, no matter how inappropriate or temporary it might be.

The critical point here is that people need to be keenly aware of where they are and who they are dealing with. Giant Bank, Inc., has its own interests first and will always pursue those interests without regard to the complex risks that will be faced by the consumer over time. This in-house bias is multiplied by the lucrative nature of selling what you have manufactured yourself. A large firm has geometrically more to gain by selling its own mutual funds. These financial incentives are compounded by the multiple layers that the firm has its hand in—from trading to research and underwriting. The large firm will generate fees at every layer of these vertical food chains. In my own research, the track records of most of these proprietary products are crushed by all the bias of the in-house resources. The house brand is overprocessed and refined by the financial firm to the point that it is usually bad for your financial health. The US government might want to consider a warning label similar to the one it requires for cigarettes!

Another force in this car dealer structure of distribution is insurance companies. Insurance companies often employ their own employees as captive sales representatives. Life insurance companies were one of the pioneers in the "career" agency system. This method of insurance distribu-tion entails an office with recruiters who spend their time hiring and training sales agents. These agents are trained and allowed only to sell the sponsor insurance company's products. This is a dicey proposition. The sales managers are motivated by the potential of receiving "overrides," which are separate layers of commission that come from the total that the client ultimately pays.

The sales pressure created in these marketing offices can be immense and can drive the salespeople to unethical or even flat-out fraudulent practices. There has been significant class action in cases where life insurance companies have gone to policy holders of their old contracts and convinced the policy holders that the "new and improved" version was to their benefit. Due to the complexity of these life insurance products, the policy holders were at a huge disadvantage and often would feel that they trusted "their" agent. A new transaction would then be entered with new costs, and, of course, commissions for the sales food chain, with little benefit to the policy holder.

Often, I find consumers who have investment plans with a huge component of life insurance. Insurance companies are in business to sell insurance, so this bias should be obvious. However, in the modern marketplace for retail investments and advice, many of these insurers have gone to great lengths to position themselves as "financial services" companies. Banks often enter into marketing agreements with insurance companies, further blurring the lines and motivations for whose interests are being served. Credit unions have either teamed with insurance companies or formed their own to cross-sell their members. The problem is that most consumers are completely oblivious to these biases and to the fact that they are being sold and not advised.

There has been much tinkering with securities laws to try to protect the consumer from this bias. The trend has been one of less restriction on the multiple lines of products that financial firms enter. The political activities of the large financial firms are legendary. Even when the regulations are strong, the marketplace is always one step ahead of the regulators. There have been many examples of companies that have paid their "advisors" higher rates of compensation to recommend the house brand. Now, there are regulations that prohibit these kinds of practices. Nevertheless, if you can make a rule, someone will find a way around it. The sad part is that you see companies that have captive employees and in-house products straining to claim there is no bias. I am convinced that there is usually a distinct bias.

Generally, the more well known the financial company, the more likely the bias toward the in-house brand. I believe that the more these companies spend on their brand recognition and marketing programs, the more they must charge the end customer. Whom else can they charge for the TV and advertising costs?

There is currently a television marketing campaign running on behalf of a large financial marketing firm. The message is not about performance, service, or processes that the company uses to help people grow their wealth. No, it is rather about helping people achieve their "dreams." The marketing includes a celebrity spokesperson and high-quality ads. I can only imagine the costs of such a campaign. It is just another example in a long line of marketing that sells the sizzle, not the boring meat and potatoes, of the process of being a successful long-term investor.

I would speculate that the "dream" marketing leads consumers into a maze of computer-generated charts about how much money they will need to fund vacations, weddings, education of grandkids, and many other wonderful and worthy goals. It is admirable to use these techniques in an effort to inspire people to invest and save. Unfortunately, after the marketing costs and profits of these large financial companies are assessed from the clients' accounts, the dreams will come up far short of reality.

Firms trying to advertise anything by image enter a very difficult if not impossible mission of communicating performance. This is a very difficult issue for all the participants in the field of financial advice. Advertising performance is complex and restricted by regulation, for good reason. Communicating past performance is essentially not done. This barrier creates endless advertising of concepts and images, much of which is dreamed up by marketing departments and advertising agencies.

Recently, I evaluated a large money management firm that was offering a program based on selecting a "goal" (such as paying for college) that it would then help achieve through its money management. I found this to be another example of concept marketing masking the very mundane but critically important aspects of quality performance in the actual money management. I had always noted that this firm had a shaky track record of performance. Instead of focusing on efforts to improve performance, the marketing department came up with a way to shift the focus to the setting of "goals." These types of conceptual gimmicks are introduced constantly and, after a couple of years, are gone into the dustbin forever.

Dealing with a financial company that offers in-house money man-agement is generally a treacherous path for the investor. Once an investor is engaged with that firm, he or she will be subject to the unique philosophy of only that firm. Often, I have found large financial marketing companies making every effort to focus on things other than quality, costs, and performance. Asset management firms will tout "risk-adjusted" performance of their money management. I have found that this is an easy shroud for asset managers to hide their shortcomings. Lousy results are justified by the notion that the firm was protecting you by taking less risk.

Whether it is the purchase of a vehicle, home furniture, or a new appliance, it is imperative to understand whether you are in a biased product dealership. There are alternatives to this vertical food chain distribution system. Consumers also need to continuously evaluate if what is being considered for purchase is actually what they want, or what they have been marketed so vigorously to desire. Let us now examine another structure that is a significant presence in today's financial landscape. I like to call it "the supermaket."

The supermarket environment creates problems that are subtle, but just as potentially damaging. As an advisor myself, I am constantly being solicited by financial product companies. By air, land, and sea … by mail, phone, fax, e-mail, and personal visit, I am inundated by salespeople and financial product marketing. Many of the financial firms that have gone away from the goal of creating their own house brands (often due to poor results) have become like a supermarket for the financial product manufacturers. Many firms simply want to be the custodian or "the shelf" for the financial products that I recommend to my clients. The management companies are then all vying behind the scenes to get to the front of the shelf—to be recommended by the marketing firms and advisors.

Some of the major discount brokerage firms have embraced this model vigorously. These firms do a nice job of offering tools and services that give access to financial products, particularly mutual funds from many different firms. The untold story here is that these mutual fund supermarkets charge for the right to be included on the menu. The message that these firms advertise heavily is that there are no transaction fees for the purchase of thousands of different mutual funds. This is true, but only funds that are willing to pay the discount firm are included in the no-transaction-fee proposition. When you evaluate these menus, you may find many good choices, along with a great number of mutual funds that should probably be avoided.

The reality is that the supermarket model can only be profitable by markups or charging for shelf space. I have concluded that most of these financial marketing firms are doing both. They are letting money manage-ment companies compete on the price they are willing to pay for shelf space. Then, the supermarket adds a markup to what the traffic and regulations will bear. The revenue that mutual funds generate can be shared with the custodian or supermarket firm. This is a murky area of the business known as "revenue sharing."

The old-line Wall Street firms are heavy participants in this supermarket concept. These firms use outside firms that are willing to pay significant "revenue sharing" as a means for profits and the appearance of objectivity. Revenue sharing is a legal practice of paying part of the asset management charge of a mutual fund to the firm that is the recordkeeper or custodian of the shares. Below is a description and disclosure that relates to revenue sharing in the offering of outside mutual funds. It is sample disclosure language that we are supposed to use to factor into our decision making:

From each fund family we offer, we seek to collect a mutual fund support fee, or what has come to be called a revenue-sharing payment. These revenue-sharing payments are in addition to the sales charges, annual distribution and service fees (referred to as "12b-1 fees"), applicable redemption fees and deferred sales charges, and other fees and expenses disclosed in the fund's prospectus fee table. Revenue-sharing payments are paid out of the investment adviser's or other fund affiliate's revenues or profits and not from the fund's assets. However, fund affiliate revenues or profits may in part be derived from fees earned for services provided to and paid for by the fund. No portion of these revenue-sharing payments to (firm name) is made by means of brokerage commissions generated by the fund.

It is also important to note that our Financial Advisors receive absolutely no additional compensation as a result of these revenue-sharing payments.

In 2008, we are charging fund families revenue-sharing fees up to a maximum per fund family of: (a) 0.09% per year ($9 per $10,000) on fixed income fund assets held by our clients, and (b) 0.12% per year ($12 per $10,000) on equity, balanced and offshore fund assets held by our clients, subject to a minimum charge of $50,000 per year per fund family, or $25,000 per year for fund families that offer five or fewer funds at (firm name) . In addition, they will be subject to volume discounting (that is, as the number of assets increases, the basis point charge for those assets will decrease).

Set forth below is a listing of the fund families from which we received revenue-sharing payments in 2007. Fund families are listed based upon the total amount of revenue-sharing payments we recognized from each fund family for 2007.

Representatives of Fund Families are, subject to the discretion of Branch Office Managers, provided access to our branch offices and Financial Advisors for educational, marketing and other promotional efforts. Although all fund families are provided with such access, some fund families devote more staff and resources to these activities and therefore may have enhanced opportunities to promote their funds to our Financial Advisors. This fact could, in turn, lead our Financial Advisors to focus on those funds when recommending mutual fund investments to our clients instead of on funds from those fund families that do not commit similar resources to education, marketing and other promotional efforts. Fund families that do not remit revenue-sharing payments typically will not be provided such access and will not participate in or receive other corporate promotional support.

There is a lot going on behind the scenes. Many financial products end up in John Q. Public's portfolio by the push of marketing fee sharing, not because of any underlying quality or integrity of the product. I think a great amount of what goes on is marketing and glitz, not research and putting the clients first. My beliefs are based on firsthand experience of being romanced for years by all sorts of mutual fund, insurance, and other financial product companies. I find that many products on these financial supermarket shelves are not there due to quality track records of performance. Beyond the marketing, there is the strong bias of fee sharing that many of the highest quality mutual funds simply do not have to pay because they can attract assets due to their long-term histories of good performance.

A strong example of this supermarket problem can be found in many variable annuities. Some of these programs offer more than 50 different sub-account investment options. In my research, I have found that a great majority of these investment options are mediocre in their historical performance. I believe that the supermarket (in this case, an insurance company) would like to offer the best money managers, but it has a higher bias to fee-sharing arrangements offered by the upstart and historically mediocre money managers out there. Variable annuities can be particularly damaging due to the fact that they lock in money with significant penalties for early withdrawal that can last as long as eight years.

Another supermarket arrangement that is particularly troubling to me is in the 401(k) arena. My professional travels have led me through numerous 401(k) evaluations. A huge portion of the plans I examine are investing in funds that have secured their place on the plan menu for reasons other than their performance history. This is an area of the highest stakes because our government, along with the Internal Revenue Service (IRS), has anointed this employer-sponsored platform as the pension of the future.

I have found many, if not the majority, of 401(k) plans to have investment choices with mediocre performance history. It is frightening to think of what is going on when you read endless accounts of consulting companies taking fees from money management companies in addition to being paid by their clients. For smaller companies that do not hire consulting firms, you have commissioned salespeople marketing to small business owners. The business owners simply want to run their business without aggravation from a retirement plan. The 401(k) provider has effectively set up a supermarket that is collecting money directly from employee paychecks. There are numerous examples of class action litigation in the area of revenue sharing in plans that seem to offer mutual funds with high costs and dubious historical performance.

401(k) participants need to be persistent and aggressive in their monitoring of the retirement plan offered by their employer. The sad reality is that most people think that one 401(k) plan is the same as the next. I find the most common perception among workers and participants in these plans is one of passive resignation that there is little they can do. There is also an implication in these plans that someone is monitoring for quality. In reality, many of these plans are financial supermarkets run by insurance companies that are negotiating with money managers for the highest fee the market will bear. These fees are then charged in ways that are not easily understood by plan participants and the result is much less money (due to poor or mediocre performance) for the average worker in the 401(k) balance.

I believe the issue of shelf space and fee arrangements is one of the most challenging problems faced by the financial services industry. How does an investor protect himself? You need to hire you own architect!

The analogy here is very powerful … When you hire an independent financial advisor (your architect), he or she can help to eliminate the car dealer dynamic. Bias can never be eliminated completely, but once you hire an independent architect, he or she can become your advocate for hire. By charging a fully disclosed fee paid directly by the client (it is not paid by any financial company), an independent advisor/architect can filter through the largest and oldest established money managers for your portfolio while keeping your money away from the companies that are paying fees simply to be on the marketer's shelf.

If you are going to build a new house (portfolio), you have a variety of choices. Let us narrow the idea down to two scenarios. The first option it to contract with your own architect/designer. You will then shop for a building site, create the design, etc., all with the assistance of your professional counsel. Location, design, and materials will all be custom chosen with the help of your architectural and design team.

The second option it to select a home in a planned development. The design is limited to the models offered by the builder and you have your choice of land, but only within the given development.

Which case is likely to yield the dream home? Certainly, both cases have pros and cons. There is great risk associated with building your own custom home. I would contend here that the independently designed property will have better value for the dollar. Your personal advisor will look for the best value in terms of design. The bricks, exterior, furnace, and plumbing are likely to be the highest value for the dollar spent. Your personal advisor would only want the best construction techniques and materials.

The tract home offering has many of these same values, but it is a closed system. The homes are designed for profitability. These large projects involve huge risk in their development and marketing costs that must be recovered from sales of the homes, just as the large financial companies have huge costs in the marketing and retail location expenses that must be paid.

There is a strong irony here that the companies that are the most widely recognized by virtue of their advertising may be some of the worst in terms of the products offered. Who is paying for all the advertising? There are many money managers and advisors who do not advertise. They have grown slowly over time through practice and refinement of the difficult job of money management.

It is imperative for an investor to understand fully who is being served by an investment strategy. Is the investment firm also in the business of investment banking? Does it have in-house money management? Is the insurance company purely striving for investment quality, or is there a bias toward risk management of the proposition? These are some of the questions an investor needs to ask.

When a firm is serving many masters, it may not be very good at any given task. In today's marketplace, it is a popular concept to "get the whole package" on "one simple bill." The bank wants to handle all your investing needs. I see tremendous bias in these types of offerings. The reality of this is that the general practitioner does not do heart surgery. Investment management and portfolio allocation is not banking. Insurance companies and banks do not have a great history in guiding the individual in his or her financial decisions. Who designed and helped sell all of the adjustable-rate mortgages that are now causing such unfortunate troubles? These large institutions tend to have large-scale costs in the development of their products and the marketing of those products. They then go out into the marketplace to recoup those costs.

There are many examples of this. Banks as financial dealerships or supermarkets are a prime example. Historically barred from the investment business, banks are now at the front in marketing to the consumer for asset management. It seems to me to reek with conflict of interest. What business is the bank really in? Grandma Bessie is now sitting with an annuity sales rep right in the lobby of the bank. The bank has cut a marketing deal with the insurance company. Now you have a completely biased situation and great potential for confusion by the consumer. Banks are obligated to warn on investment products that they are "not FIDC insured." I hope that this warning works better at protecting people than the similar warning has for cigarettes!

Another case in point is the traditional wire house or stock brokerage firm. Was it ever really possible that the broker was earning profits for his clients? It has been shown time and again how that model of investment advice had a huge bias toward trading and the generation of commissions. I think the descendents of those firms are now supermarket-type institutions that continuously introduce complex investment concepts (e.g., hedge funds, separate account management, private equity, market neutral funds, exchange-traded funds (ETFs), and other concepts) that may prove unfortunate for investors in the future.

Independent financial advisors can help filter through all these different options on behalf of their clients. Basing the financial advisory relationship on strict fiduciary ethical standards with all costs to the client fully disclosed creates a significant structural advantage for the investor. The independent advisor's only motivation is to help the investor gain financial strength. Within the context of a fiduciary relationship, the advisor can set about creating efficient, cost-effective, and rational strategies. The client and advisor can each be seated at the same side of the table, with only the interests of the client's portfolio quality and growth as the measure of success.

401(k) Reality

"It's clearly a budget. It's got a lot of numbers in it."

George W. Bush

A Tax Code provision created in 1978 and formalized in 1981 that was initiated to allow corporate executives the choice of deferring bonuses from tax has become the foundation of the modern retirement plan. Now that pensions are becoming an extinct species of financial asset for most of us, we will be left with the executive supplement. I confidently predict that this accidental design has created a huge underfunding problem for the vast majority of 401(k) participants in the United States. The 401(k) was never intended to be the single source of a worker's retirement savings!

Traditionally, an employer would contribute between 6 percent and 8 percent of its payroll toward an employee pension plan. Nowadays, the maximum employer contribution to a 401(k) tops out at around 5 percent of payroll, and often ranges at 2 percent down to zero. The 401(k) has provided cover for employers who seek to eliminate retirement obligations to a huge portion of the American work force. Some corporations are more generous, but this trend has created what I see as a great illusion among average workers that "one day I'll retire with my 401(k)." The golden era of retirement that has existed in the United States for the last 30 years or so will be quite different now that there will be no base pension for people to rely on.

Recent studies have shown that the average 401(k) balance of American workers over age 60 is under $40,000! This shocking lack of preparedness is a sad indication of the folly that is the 401(k). This shortfall is a mirror of what we are now experiencing with cascading Medicare liabilities that will threaten the financial viability of the federal government of the United States. Generations of workers from the golden age of American worker benefits were led to believe in the magic genie of lifetime employer-paid health care. Now, these masses of retirees are being loaded onto the federal safety nets of Medicare and Medicaid.

I often wonder who will help these people with any level of retirement income, let alone the resources for health care into the seventh and eighth decades of life. People have remained passive and under an illusion that there is a social safety net that will care for them.

The implications of this restructuring of benefits and compensation to American workers are greatly misunderstood. Workers simply do not recognize the impact of how they allocate and how much they contribute to their 401(k) plan. Some studies have shown that no less than 25 percent of workers will never even enroll in their plan. Retirement assets have become the obligation of the employee. Many would argue that the ever changing nature of the workplace and work force requires the flexibility and portability that 401(k) plans create. These arguments have greatly missed the crucial issue … how will a worker earning $60,000 per year ever a cumulate the $750,000 to $1,000,000 that will be necessary to create a consistent income in retirement?

In my experience, the answer is that most individuals will be grossly deficient in their retirement savings when that critical time arrives to stop working. There are a large number of factors converging to create this glaring weakness that so many seem to ignore. The lack of responsibility placed on employers for the retirement funding of the worker is the political reality that exists, and it is unlikely to change. What bothers me more is the lack of quality in most 401(k) plans that I examine, the lack of concern in most workers for their 401(k), and the sheer ignorance and passivity that I witness in most individual's retirement planning diligence.

If we look at the model of employer-provided health insurance as another area where the employer has taken responsibility for the well-being of workers, I am not optimistic. The notion that employers will compete with each other by offering the best benefit package is something that I rarely witness in reality. The employer is usually looking to limit or reduce costs in its health insurance or 401(k) plan package. In this era of intense global economic competition, US companies carry a great cost burden that many foreign companies have never faced. The discussion of health care costs is incredibly complex. The essence of our lesson here as investors is that we must expect that there will be no one there to pay these costs, and that we must make every effort to accumulate a large reserve during our working years to protect our health and retirement income.

It seems to be an obvious conflict of interest for the employer to be expected to search out the best programs versus grind down the costs to itself. The sad reality is that these health care and retirement packages have gotten more and more complex, and it is difficult for a worker to distinguish the level of quality of his or her benefits. Once again, the opaque realm of financial complexity shows itself and I believe that results are going to be far short of what most people anticipate.

It has become standard practice for a single financial product company to be the 401(k) provider for a given group of employees. This dynamic has been driven by extreme complexity in the Internal Revenue Service (IRS) rules that govern retirement plans. Financial companies want to have exclusive access to a given group of workers so that monitoring of all the data is easier. It seems that today's massive computer power would be able to offer people a choice. A great solution that could improve the costs and quality of these group retirement plans would be to offer choices among different financial companies. Competition is the only way that better products will ultimately be offered to the end user/investor.

Unfortunately, competition is not the norm. Once an employer contracts with a 401(k) provider, the process of competitive forces is stymied by the great effort and time required to change all the participants to a new plan. 401(k) plans are the ultimate financial supermarket. A monopoly is created plan by plan for one of the largest blocks of financial assets in the US. Company by company, these 401(k) fiefdoms are created. Once the mutual fund or insurance company secures the 401(k) contract for a given company, it is the employer's fiduciary responsibility to make sure that the plan is doing the best for its participants. I find with almost every midsize or small employer plan that I review, the owners of the company are not doing much of a job as plan fiduciary and trustee. Many business owners do not have a clue about their fiduciary responsibility. Business operators are usually immersed in the daily operational practices of running their firm. Many of these people see the 401(k) as another burdensome employee benefit and they seek to minimize the time they spend so that they can tend to all the responsibilities of the core business.

Many plans that I review have very strange mutual fund options included on their menu of choices. Often, the plan choices are limited to in-house fund choices that are proprietary to the particular mutual fund or insurance company. Another common fund that will show up on 401(k) plan menus is one that has fees paid to the plan provider for allowing it to get on the menu. These fees are known as "revenue sharing." Currently, a number of significant class action lawsuits are proceeding against these defects and costs that drain away the value that can be obtained by workers.

There are all kinds of arcane IRS and Department of Labor rules that are supposed to protect and enhance these plans for workers. One of my favorite examples is the huge binder that I often see presented in the annual review meeting. This is a collection of documents that represent the history of the plan. These collections include the plan document, summary plan description, form 5500, amendments, annual reports, annual testings of the plan, annual deferral percentage, and many other arcane documents that are rarely looked at after their creation. I often notice that these binders are filled with things that have very little bearing on the quality of the plan or the plan's actual investment performance. Mostly, I see these endless recordkeeping requirements as worker protection and job creation for accounting and retirement plan administrative firms.

All of this complexity is created by the simple notion of protecting the worker. There is a built-in bias that people who are more highly compensated will take greater advantage of the tax deferral and long-term benefits of the 401(k) rules. This fact of life has spawned an ever expanding set of rules with the objective of forcing the employer to make sure that there is no "discrimination" in the plans. The plans have to be tested by a recordkeeping company every year to make sure that all the rules are followed.

When these rules were enacted, many deferrals of higher earning employees were disallowed. Instead of having the desired effect of motivating employers to provide incentives to lower income individuals on a given payroll (which is often impossible due to the fact that at a certain level of pay, it is simply impossible to "save" for the future), the discrimination rules simply reduced the deferrals that were being made to plans by the more highly compensated workers. Some plans certainly increased their employer matching, but most of what I have witnessed has a match rate of a paltry 3 percent or 4 percent of an employee's pay, up to a cap of $500 to $2,000 per year.

Once again, the law of unintended consequences rears its ugly head, with the employer matching contributions only up to the required amount, and greatly added complexity along with the additional costs of recordkeeping and compliance. These discrimination rules, having such a negative impact, were then amended to include what is known as a "safe harbor" 401(k) plan. Yes, now employers had a safe harbor from the storm of endless complexity! The terminology is quite ironic. These safe harbor plans must offer a basic match of 4 percent of an employee's pay (there are actually variations of this rule, but let us use the 4 percent match as a general estimate). This allows any highly compensated employee to defer to the legal limit without regard to discrimination or even the need to run annual tests.

The lunacy of the IRS and the US Congress is demonstrated here. Your government cannot motivate people with low income to invest through tax breaks! Low-income individuals may receive little or no benefit at all from tax deferral. Low-wage earners in general are strapped to get by month to month and are rarely interested in the concept of investing for the future, even if there are federal tax credits given to them to induce saving. These individuals are also rarely interested in tying money into long-term commitments due to the uncertainty of their year-to-year or even month-to-month income. Thus, unless the government wants to force employers to actually contribute significant amounts to a given worker's retirement, all these arcane 401(k) rules simply complicate the plans for those among us who can and do want to save for the future.

These comments regarding low-wage earners sound quite cynical. I would posit that these low-income individuals are the exact people that social security, Medicare, and Medicaid were created to serve. Those among us who are never so lucky as to achieve the education or skills that will allow for significant accumulation should be assisted by those who can. The irony here is that the endless tube of legislative sausage (Employee Retirement Income Security Act (ERISA), Pension Protection Act, etc.) that continues to be forced down the US economy's throat only creates more bureaucracy and costs to the retirement planning options that earnest savers have to choose from.

These complicated manipulations by the US Congress are but one example of how a noble idea of trying to help low-income workers save has morphed into a morass of complex rules that end up benefiting no one and creating significant additional costs and complexity. Employee education, continuous review of plan options, and ongoing financial guidance are a few elements that should exist in theory, but are rarely found in the real world. In my years in the field working with plan participants, I have found little that is done that really enhances the workers' chances of having a sufficient income source when they retire. It will take a balance of $900,000 to $1,100,000 to produce the $40,000 to $50,000 that seems to me to be the minimum income to live a secure retirement. We cannot rely on employers to assure that these plans are working well for employees. The owners are busy these days simply trying to stay in business. It has been my experience that only a very small percentage of people take their 401(k) at all seriously.

401(k) loan provisions have been created in plans under a theory that people might save more if they know access to the money is available in an emergency. This was not the case when people had a growing pension benefit as they worked through their career. If you had a pension plan, you could only get to it at retirement and that protected you from yourself. Now, when people live beyond their means, they can take a loan against their 401(k). If you allow people to borrow for today's needs against the future, a significant percentage will do so. This access to retirement assets prior to retirement is another great unknown in the new age of the 401(k)-based retirement era. This "live for the now" dynamic is built into our modern culture. I have often heard people say they would never put money into something that they cannot "get at."

Once a participant borrows from the plan, he or she will then begin mandatory payments back to the account, so no harm done, right? Well, it will certainly reduce the amount that worker can contribute. These mandatory repayments also can be disrupted if a worker leaves the job before repaying a 401(k) loan. I am not under the illusion here that we should try to design plans to help save participants from themselves. I do think that every effort must be made to educate and even coerce people into saving and investing in a systematic way—until it hurts. It will hurt a lot more when people are older and have no way to catch up and then are forced to live on a very limited fixed income.

Another difficult reality for me as an advisor is that 401(k) plans do not pay me to help my clients with guidance and advice. There are fees in these plans, but they go to the individuals who set up the plan, again giving them a monopoly on all the participant money in the plan, regardless of whether they make an effort to help the workers. I find that most plans do not have active advisors. The broker or insurance sales rep who has a relationship with the business owner can usually be found on the golf course or at a fancy restaurant entertaining his owner clients. If the participants need help, they can go to the web site. Sadly, many participants never keep up with their plan options.

Recently, there has been a significant movement to add provisions aimed at enhancing plan features for participants. One of these allows employers to automatically enroll new employees in a plan when they are hired. The concept here is aimed to force people to opt out proactively if they do not want to save. I find this to be at odds with rules that allow many employers to avoid any matching contribution if a given participant does not enroll in the plan. Most midsize and small employers actually have barriers to plan entry, such as a requirement for a given worker to have one year of service before he or she become eligible to participate in the plan!

Along the line of auto enrollment is the provision to make an investment election for that participant (since so many have been too lazy to do so themselves). And what will that election be? A target date mutual fund … that new and unproven concept! Why not just give that employee a small pension? The 401(k) rules have become so complex that the plans may be coming full circle back to the age of the guaranteed pension with one slight difference—much less money put in by employers.

If we step back to try to see the big picture, it is not very promising. The plan requires workers to defer their own money, invest it wisely over the long run, and then make prudent decisions during the payout phase in order to safely fund their retirement. When you ponder this idea, it doesn't sound likely, but that is the reality that we face.

Many things can be done to help all workers in this process. There should be open competition for the dollars that people defer for their future. This competition would force companies to strive for cost efficiency and greater quality over time. All plans should allow for a financial advisor to directly assist plan participants for a reasonable fee. A provision in the Tax Code should allow for high limits of tax-deferred saving for long-term medical needs that could be also used for retirement.

Media Frenzy

"If you don't read the newspaper, you are uninformed; if you do read the newspaper, you are misinformed."

Mark Twain

"If it bleeds, it leads." The modern model of newspaper and television follows a philosophy that causes our news to be focused on many things that do not seem very helpful to the average citizen. Witness your local newscast night after night with live coverage of the latest mugging, murder, or horrible accident. I am not sure who benefits from all this information. It seems that we have been trained to be interested in murder trials, car accidents, and spectacular events that have a very low probability of ever happening to a given individual. I feel compassion for those individuals and families that face these tragic events, but I do not know how it benefits me to know about them.

After the latest liquor store robbery story, what comes next on our local news broadcast? The television news formula usually produces a human interest story. I am often touched be the accomplishments or suffering of someone in our local area. It presents a chance for this person to be recognized for his or her work in a charitable cause. These human interest stories can be worthy of our attention. The huge defect here is that in the context of infotainment, there is never any follow-up. Week after week, we see another story of people struggling with disease, losing their home or job, or some other terrible trauma. It is always a new story. Last week's flood victims are cast aside for this week's new disaster. We become numb to all the information because there is no continuity. This is our cultural attention span, or rather our attention deficit, that exists and is made worse by the stream of television and newspapers that have no allegiance except to their advertising stream.

Next, we have the weather. Now it is time for predictions. I am often amazed by how each news outlet wants to impress us with its high-powered weather forecasting technology, like "Doppler 9000 HD" or whatever the outlet wants to call it. The fact is, all I need to know is usually a basic forecast for my day. Just let me know if I need my sweater or umbrella. Please don't try to make believe that you can tell if it will rain this Saturday, when it is only Monday.

It is comical that with all the fancy computer technology weathercasters never talk about the accuracy of their predictions. Hmmm … I wonder, could it be because you really cannot predict the weather beyond 36 hours or so with any accuracy? Folks, I am here to tell ya, the weatherman is not a high-tech wizard with a crystal ball. Once you go out past 24, or maybe 36, hours into the future, you can flip a coin as to the true accuracy of the weather report.

Up next we have sports. Now we can really get to stuff that doesn't matter. Why does the local news still devote time to sports at all? Entire cable channels are dedicated to sports news. The over-exposure of sports is staggering if I look back over the changes I have witnessed in the last 20 years. I can hardly wait to hear about the new $5 million per year contract for a football coach for our local university team! Our culture has created a market demand that makes athletes and even coaches into some of the highest earners in the food chain. The endless volume of games, analysis, and reporting is constantly being shoved down our throats like it really matters. I am the first one to enjoy a good sports contest, but sadly the endless over-expansion has driven the meaning out of most athletic events.

There is a horrible message for young people in the aggrandizement and hero worship of athletics. It is a message that says you can do this too. You can come up from nothing and become rich and attain one of the most highly valued places in our culture. Just keep working on throwing the ball. Rarely do you see the stories of all the people who spend their youth dreaming that they can become a professional ball player, only to come up short. This is also another example of the pie-in-the-sky mentality of American culture. Parents all over suburbia have their children taking private hitting lessons from a baseball coach in the hope that the child can one day get a scholarship or even go pro. What ever happened to moving lawns and delivering the newspaper to save and learn a work ethic?

Our hero-worshiping culture is rearing generations of dreamers who believe in athletics as a profession. There is very little balance in the messages that young people get from our powerful televised media. The misleading nature of this hero worship is a big factor in the decline of our youth's work ethic and the scholarship level in this country. Take a look next time you visit a local high school or university. There is a strong trend toward building colossal football stadiums and facilities. How does this relate to our educational system here in the United States? As government spending on research is continually cut, you can just relax and go see a game!

Athletic pursuits are a wonderful part of life. I think that it is critical for us all to take care of our physical being, and athletic activity is a critical component of our well-being. Unfortunately, I think the messages of hero worship that are broadcast have infected our culture with an over-hyped and extremely unrealistic view of what is important.

The newspaper and television media in the United States are a mirror of the junk food mentality and culture that we must try to make sense of. The public is constantly bombarded with more and more information that has less and less importance. In fact, the nature and substance of the information seems to lead in the very opposite direction from where we need to go. These infotainment-focused media outlets are significant drivers of what I see directly reflected in the financial habits of individuals and families. The mainstream news and media in general mirror the structural bias found when observing the subset that is the financial media.

The structural bias that I want to emphasize here is not only the focus on infotainment over substance, but also the lack of continuity. Continuity in our information is critically important. There are many great and talented people doing high-level work in the news media. I have the utmost respect for them. The problem here, once again, is what the media system has become in jumping from one enticing story to the next. The media are often vilified for having an agenda, or creating problems in what they emphasize. I do not subscribe to the media as villain argument at all. The problem is the lack of continuity. The follow-up is very sporadic or not at all. Issues that seem blindingly important for a week or so may never be covered again.

There was a recent story in the national television media regarding the conditions in Veterans Administration hospitals. There was a great scandal that soldiers who came back from the war in Iraq in need of care were facing neglect and frustration in the resources available. This was such an important story on so many levels, but it has now disappeared from the media radar. Did this story help? I hope so. We must recognize that as citizens, and investors, we need to take great care in creating continuity in our information stream.

The financial media have these very same sensation-focused characteristics. The more you listen, the less you may ultimately learn. The excitement of the "Top 10 Stocks to Buy Now" on the cover of the latest pop financial magazine is unlikely to benefit your portfolio's future. The current crisis in the cost of oil or the value of the dollar may seem riveting, but it will not help in calibrating your money management and allocation selections.

In the financial news, excitement (it bleeds, it leads) is usually generated by large swings in the market or financial fears that are recited and repeated until the next more exciting crisis comes along. Once again, the mundane and slow building process of eating your financial vegetables and creating fiscal fitness does not make for compelling television.

Financial media are filled with infotainment just like any other news. I find more and more weight being given to the entertainment component. There are now multiple TV programs featuring individual stock picking. Excited callers are heard raving about the trades that they have made. I never see the performance tracking of the picks of the host or discussions of fundamental principles for long-term success. The mundane nuts and bolts of asset allocation, manager selection, and long-term patient investing are rarely seen. These types of education and long-term strategic planning issues simply do not make the cut. The likelihood of successful portfolio managers giving away their stock selections is nil. The profitability of managing money is much higher than the wages of a television personality.

Take a moment here to remember that the television medium is arguably the most powerful force in information distribution and opinion formation in our modern American culture. People are going to accept the information they are being fed given enough repetition. The message communicated by these stock-picking programs that the average individual can trade in and out of stocks for profit is a ludicrous and highly destructive message that is being carried in all sorts of ways. An endless stream of meaningless noise is everywhere in the televised media structure. The news crawl (a throwback to the tickers of the old days of stock trading) as a constant on the bottom of every news broadcast is symbolic of the noise stream. Take a look at the typical cable news outlet and watch the crawl spew streams of irrelevance, like sports scores or an update on British royalty.

The stock crawl on a financial broadcast outlet is in itself an irrelevant tool. It is a symbol that the financial cable channels use to create a milieu of financial excitement. The modern technology of real-time trade reporting at your desktop computer renders a screen crawl obsolete. Why does this information take up valuable screen space? It is there to send the viewer a message of excitement. No serious investors are using that information

Television has one objective, and that is to sell advertising. The programming is not there for any other reason. The shows produced live or die by attracting viewers and advertising revenue, not by a grading of their quality. The excitement that can be generated is the weighted criterion when television executives make their programming choices. This premise of excitement above all else is exemplified by the financial news channels use of the "breaking news" concept. The message here is that we can all think like professional traders and monitor economic reports, political events, and the like for use in our moment-to-moment decision making. This dynamic runs completely opposite to the long-term mindset that is so very critical to intelligent investor decision making.

The idea that an amateur investor can quickly react as news "breaks" and make financial decisions is insane. There are teams of sophisticated traders running large pools of money all over the world. They will react to news much more quickly than any desktop stock jockey can.

Media sources that are subscription based are much more important for intelligent investors looking to refine their understanding of what is happening around them. Keeping current with beacons of credible information such as the *Wall Street Journal*, the *New York Times*, *Business Week*, the *Economist,* and more technical financial journal outlets is one way to gather understanding. Of course, there is an entire shadow group of pseudo-financial publication that I consider "pop" money publications that offer bottomless rivers of "hot list" content that can be very damaging to the unsuspecting consumer.

The noise of the modern media is deafening and defeats the power of our modern communications technology. Noise can be defined as everything outside of the actual message. The essential grist for serious investors is deep research, consistent periodic review, long-term strategic vision, and, most of all, patience. This will not sell many magazines or make for good TV.

Noise is primarily what you get through many print and televised channels. Witness three reporters working on a story of this month's unemployment report. One month's economic report number is a great example of meaningless noise that will be forgotten within hours or days. Yet here are reporters on the scene, expending time and energy about last month's unemployment stats, retail sales, or gasoline prices. The sheer scale of resources devoted to these small technical events is shocking. This is an example of the over-the-top nature of today's news media and the excessive noise that is continually generated. The more of this noise we are exposed to, the less energy we will have to seek out and contemplate important information.

The idea that what is exciting is worthy of our attention and end-less analysis causes our energy to be directed at many of the wrong things. I harbor no illusion that we will all sit and watch C-Span, PBS, or other long documentary-type programming constantly in order to get to the real data and essence of what is going on. Much of what appears in those types of outlets is also unimportant. To understand our world and our chance for a higher quality of information and decision making requires a clear understanding of where and how the information that is broadcast originates.

There is a very important consideration here when consuming financial media: Is the source a professional speaker or a financial professional? Those commentators who are strictly speakers and not professional money managers need to be recognized as such; they are paid to speak, not necessarily to be competent. Rarely do elite financial professionals emerge into the public domain and reveal their strategy, tactics, or anything else. Many managers of mutual funds or insurance companies are available all the time while they seek publicity and free advertising for a particular fund or firm. I have often noticed many managers of extremely small or start-up mutual funds on television. I imagine they have a public relations firm working hard to find opportunities for public speaking engagements of all types.

There exists another public commentary that is pervasively produced by an army of financial journalists. I am sure that many of these professional writers are quite competent … as journalists. It is rare to get novel or useful information from most of these people. Most of what I see in print is recycled, idealistic, and generic information. The task of the financial journalist is difficult if the goal is to consistently produce innovative, useful material. There is a small, elite group of journalists who are often out doing the hard, investigative work while the rest of the writers recycle generic frivolity or become outlets for financial companies seeking publicity.

This dynamic is very common in books and other print media. Endless titles with "millionaire" in them are produced. This kind of snake oil has been around for a very long time. I have found very little magic in these types of books. Why talk about the simple fundamentals that we all can incorporate when you can skip all the hard work and become a millionaire fast? Use of the word "millionaire" or "rich" in the title of a book or seminar or other system that is sold to the public has been around for a long time, and it seems to be especially prevalent now. Why is this happening? I would say that it is just another example of how our culture is focused on the extreme. It is not likely that the secret to riches is finally being revealed in any book.

Financial magazines are great offenders of practicality with their endless sensationalism. Although there is much useful information out there, you will find lots of hype about hot managers or stocks. This fast-food mentality is found in financial periodicals at every turn. Investing in the extra-crispy portfolio with gravy is not going to be good for your portfolio's health, but it will sure seem exciting enough to buy the magazine. Who can resist reading about retiring when you are 45 years old? The new and exciting, as we have discussed, are potentially the most dangerous. I do think that the junk food analogy is perfect in so many cases in the financial print media.

One example of this dynamic is seen when a mutual fund or money manager has racked up very high results. Currently, investments in China, commodities, and gas and oil have been some of the highest returning areas. This focus on the recent short-term winners causes many to make the classic mistake of buying high after the results have been good.

The hottest performing fund of the year is something that should be evaluated with extreme caution. Usually, mutual funds that rack up the best track record over a three- or even five-year period are heavily concentrated and have taken high levels of risk relative to the top 200 fund universe. This does not stop the pop financial magazines from publishing endless lists of "10 funds to buy now" and other such misleading and possibly risky advice. The tracking of these recommendations from year to year is rare. I have never seen any of these financial magazines follow up with a tracking of how an investor would have fared if he or she allocated to the top fund every year. Using a hot fund list is probably the worst way to select mutual funds.

There is another force at work here in these types of media. The underlying message is that, with a little help from the show, book, or magazine, you will be on your way to investing success. The various media outlets and personalities have a huge stake in creating the notion that they are dispensing guidance and important information for investors to use in making decisions. With a magazine subscription, ticket to a seminar, and a set of how-to DVDs, you will be on the road to financial freedom. It is very easy to preach the notion that there is some type of financial secret sauce.

Hard work, patience, and sacrifice are not things that people end up doing because they read it in a book or see it on TV. This realm of print media has a primary agenda of convincing people that they can pretty much do it themselves with a subscription, a little research, and a few hours of review per month. That may be the case for a small group of diligent investors, but a positive result is unlikely for the mass market that most of these media are aimed at.

Diligent analysis of how to employ our money and our time is a concept that speaks for itself. The excitement of short-term events, changes in interest rates, unemployment reports, and other minutia has very little relevance for most investors. I often chuckle to myself as I watch a countdown in minutes, seconds, and tenths of a second to some piece of economic data like it is the launch of some type of space-craft. The primary goal of covering the "events" is to keep the viewer so that more advertising can be sold.

A thorough discussion of mass media must include commentary on the Internet. The Internet is an incredible tool for investors to use in the research, tracking, and performance measurement of portfolios. It is also an unfiltered universe of massive quantities of data, much of which is of dubious quality and origin. The sheer mass of information does present quite a dilemma. The Internet has completely removed any barriers to entry for anyone looking to pontificate about all matters financial and otherwise. This lack of barrier, filtration, editing, or fact checking is fraught with opportunity for fraud, exploitation, and manipulation of many less aware people.

There exists a colossal media stream known as message or bulletin boards. These are purely Internet-based phenomena that are ripe for fraud and manipulation. We have seen many cases of chief executive officers, traders, and stock promoters creating false online identities and spreading positive or negative rumors that can build up their own firms or denigrate competitors. People can log in to a message board and say whatever comes to mind without even identifying themselves.

There is a high likelihood that any investor with meaningful insight would not be blathering on the web, but would most likely keep the information to himself.

The advancing sophistication of tools, interfaces, and available data can be incredibly useful. The risk is that most of these tools will encourage thinking like a trader as opposed to a long-term-minded investor. As investors are presented with all kinds of tools formerly only accessed by professionals, I think we will see more and more misuse of those very tools. Imagine for a moment that we were to give weekend do-it-yourselfers a fully equipped shop of woodworking tools. Without the proper training, apprentice time, and experience, I think we would witness a lot of accidents and even missing fingers.

The trading tools that can be delivered at a cost of $9.95 per trade are quite astounding. The Internet has driven delivery costs close to zero. The information streams that online brokerage firms are delivering to amateur investors create a powerful illusion that you too can sit and trade all day in the big market game. These tools are likely to deceive many into believing that they can compete with the pros.

As our modern society continuously becomes more and more complex, it is extremely important for investors to recognize what they know, and, even more importantly, what they don't know. As I have mentioned repetitively, complexity can be a demon that leads to outcomes we could never predict or understand. The complexity created by this endless stream of noise that has very little meaning causes much damage to the unenlightened masses. Recognition of the fact that most of this information is irrelevant is a critical step in our education as prudent investors and citizens of this planet.

Here are strategic thinking points to help you traverse the complex investment world:

1. Mass media are generally infotainment and must be looked upon with a cynical eye.

2. Continuity is critical to the way investors receive their information. Sources for ongoing evaluation and follow-up such as newsletters

and other subscription-based services are the best resources for ongoing information.

3. Subscription services such as the *Wall Street Journal*, the *New York Times, Forbes, Fortune, Business Week, Value Line, Morningstar*, and other publications are vastly superior to advertising-based pop infotainment.

Composure during seemingly dramatic events is critical for investors. As the media shape a sensational vision of many of the tragic stories of our modern world, long-term investors must remain calm and dispas-sionate. Military invasions, terrorist attacks, and natural disasters are all a part of what will prevent many from ever becoming owners of the quality investments that are the key to creating financial strength. Most of these events prove to have only temporary impacts as markets swing on short- term news, only to sober up to the long-term value of quality company ownership through the benefit of time and perspective.

The Magic of 10 Percent

"Too many people are thinking of security instead of opportunity. They seem to be more afraid of life than death."

James F. Bymes

Over the last 70 years, a diversified portfolio of large company stocks has returned nearly 10 percent per year on average. As we have previously discussed, once an investment plan reaches its fifteenth or twentieth birthday, the compounding of returns becomes very rewarding. There is a point at which a successful investor begins to really believe and trust in the process of long-term thinking and investing. Loyalty to one's investments forms and allows the portfolio to occupy a position of trust and quiet belief in the wisdom of long-term ownership. Trust and confidence in the ownership principle becomes ever more critical as we enter the phase of income production. It is now time for our investments to pay us back with regular monthly income.

This ownership belief will be particularly critical as a household seeks to keep pace with inflation risk throughout retirement. Historically, the common wisdom has been that as we age, a greater percentage of our portfolio should be held in fixed-income investments. The common rule of thumb for asset allocation has been to subtract your age from 100 and the result should be held in equity investments. Thus, at age 30 we should have 70 percent of our portfolio in stocks, and at 70 years old, only 30 percent of the portfolio should be in ownership-type vehicles.

This common "wisdom" can be a very costly strategic principle to incorporate into an investor's asset allocation. Higher allocation of fixed investments will certainly produce more short-term stability, but the long-run risk of inflation is always lurking. There is a critical issue here with the recent popularity of "target date" products. The paramount question is what the allocation will be after the target date has passed. Many of these products on the market currently become income funds with very high allocations to fixed income after the crucial date has passed.

With the equity/owner investor philosophy firmly in our hearts, we can begin to think about how our portfolio will ultimately go to work and begin to provide income while still retaining a healthy allocation of equity-based investments. Traditional thinking in financial planning works from the premise that as we get older, a gradual adjustment to greater portions of fixed-income instruments in the portfolio is prudent. I do not subscribe to this way of thinking. While I generally do not advocate 100 percent equities for people in their fifth decade and beyond, I do feel that much higher allocations to the ownership side of the portfolio is of great importance. These higher equity allocations will cause more volatility and the process will not be easy. We need to recognize that it will be difficult to maintain equity allocations of 60 percent to 70 percent. The market cycles are very scary on the downside, no matter how much we believe in ownership and the long-term rewards of equity investing.

The critical issue with the task of income generation in retirement is: How much income can an investor take per year? The asset allocation rule of thumb (100 – investor age) does not address this crucial point. Take the example of a retiree with a portfolio balance of $200,000. How much income can be taken? A rate of income at 5 percent will yield $10,000 per year before taxes. An allocation of 70 percent equities is unlikely to yield the full 10 percent, but it can hopefully average 6 percent to 8 percent per year. This could allow the investor's core principal to grow over the course of retirement by achieving a growth rate in the portfolio that is higher than the withdrawal rate.

At the point in life when a rational investor decides to retire, I think that there is a mindset that visualizes a wall. I see this often in individuals approaching retirement. On the other side of the retirement wall, everything will be different. The change from working life to retirement is quite dramatic, but our investments do not know this. Inflation does not stop because we have now retired.

It is important to see that a person who lives to age 65 can easily live another 20 or even 30 years. It can be very costly to become increasingly conservative and loaner minded as retirement approaches.

Let's examine a hypothetical $200,000 portfolio that we will now begin to use to pay retirement income.

   4% average return retirement portfolio (figure 10-1)
   5% annual withdrawal rate of year-end value

Figure 10-1

Year	Investment	Withdrawal	Total Value
1	$200,000	$10,000	$197,818
5	0	$9,597	$189,198
10	0	$9,077	$178,949
15	0	$8,586	$169,255
20	0	$8,120	$160,086

   6% average return retirement portfolio (figure 10-2)
   5% annual withdrawal rate of year-end value

Figure 10-2

Year	Investment	Withdrawal	Total Value
1	$200,000	$10,000	$201,728
5	0	$10,393	$208,583
10	0	$10,836	$217,481
15	0	$11,298	$226,758
20	0	$11,780	$236,430

   8% average return retirement portfolio (figure 10-3)
   5% annual withdrawal rate of year-end value

Figure 10-3

Year	Investment	Withdrawal	Total Value
1	$200,000	$10,000	$205,638
5	0	$11,550	$235,924
10	0	$12,892	$263,333
15	0	$14,791	$302,115
20	0	$16,969	$346,609

   10% average return retirement portfolio (figure 10-4)

   5% annual withdrawal rate of year-end value

Figure 10-4

Year	Investment	Withdrawal	Total Value
1	$200,000	$10,000	$209,550
5	0	$12,133	$252,129
10	0	$15,289	$317,719
15	0	$19,266	$400,371
20	0	$24,278	$504,525

Figures shown are hypothetical and not predictive of future results. Current and future results may be lower or higher than those shown. Share prices and returns will vary, so you may lose money. Investing for short periods makes losses more likely. Investments are not FDIC-insured, nor are they deposits of or guaranteed by a bank or any other entity.

The power of the additional annual returns creates significant increases in portfolio value after 15- and 20-year periods. This simple mathematical comparison should be a wake-up call for those who continue to advocate conservatism in retirement portfolios. Generating 10 percent returns in retirement is not likely, but as we can see, it will be greatly rewarding if a portfolio can generate 6 percent to 8 percent for an investor in retirement.

Not for a moment do I delude myself that this will be an easy task over the next 15 or 20 years. In fact, if you had told me that there would be an October 1987 Black Monday, a junk bond debacle of 1989, Iraq Wars 1 and 2, the technology bubble collapse of 2000, Y2K, and 9/11 ... I would not believe it possible to be rewarded as a long-term equity investor. Surprisingly, the last 20-year time frame has been reasonably good for moderate mutual fund investors. The owner investor should set out to find quality equity investments to hold through all kinds of economic environments and rise above the short-term challenges in exchange for the building of financial strength through the long span of retirement.

In my daily practice I have seen many individuals who are overly conservative in late career and early retirement. It is critical to have a growing portfolio from which we can draw a rising income. The increasing financial demands in one's seventh and eighth decades of life cannot be addressed by fixed-income investing.

I often try to educate overly conservative retirees on these issues and it always comes back to one question: Is my investment guaranteed? No. To reach for the power of 10 percent returns, we will have no guarantees, and fluctuation will be a constant. The charts in figures 10-1through 10-4 look obvious, but the path will be filled with future scares and manias. These challenges will be scary during the down years. The fact that there are quality mega mutual funds with good 20-year track records will be of little comfort when the market in down 8 percent to 11 percent or even more during a recession and we need to continue taking income while the portfolio declines.

As we have learned, the risk to the fixed investor is the quiet erosion of value through inflation. The slow rust-like effects of loss of purchasing power will only be apparent much later. It will then be too late and those conservative "safe" loaners will be counting on the cost of living increases to their social security checks to make up the difference in gasoline, grocery, and medical costs.

The main goal for retirees is income security and lifestyle protection. The assets need to be managed prudently for the retiree. The wonderful thing about an ownership strategy is that it can be inherited readily by the subsequent generation, with little modification. The inherited portfolios of my clients' children are simply rebalanced and adapted to the needs of the next generation. I have watched with sadness as many great people who have been my clients pass away. In the cases where I have been able to continue to work with the clients' children, I have found great satisfaction in watching the legacy of ownership continue.

Over a lifetime of investing, the true achievement is the wisdom of the value long-term ownership. With prudent diversification, patience, and courage, equity owners can average returns of 7 percent to 9 percent in retirement. The risk of inflation over the course of a long retirement is the greatest risk for those who live a very long life. The only prudent way to manage the specter of inflation is to continue to see the big picture of the long term and to plan on living a very long life.

Becoming Rich

"If stock market experts were so expert, they would be buying stock, not selling advice."

Norman Augustine

An endless stream of books address the "secrets to becoming rich." I have never seen references to these types of publications when I read about the background of the wealthiest people in the world. I have yet to see anyone ranked in the top 400 list cite the reading of "Become a Millionaire" or some such garbage as an inspiration or source of knowledge.

Life-changing wealth does not come about through a how-to book or process. I believe it is a combination of ambition, skill, intelligence, and luck. There is no secret formula, and if there were, no one would be writing a book about it. The current wave of television programming and books with millionaire or billionaire in the title truly makes me laugh. Who is the audience for the same old recycled ideas of no money down real estate, stock trading systems, or sacrificing that daily cup of fancy coffee as the path to wealth?

Those who have the great ability and good fortune to become truly wealthy usually get that way without the pursuit of wealth as their primary focus. It is the vision of a service or product idea that is the focus of those who achieve financial greatness. Passion for a particular goal is a common trait among those who achieve massive wealth. The endless stream of financial self-help books is simply an exploitation of the dreams of the masses.

Many among us are motivated to become strong financially. The dream of riches is one of the most powerful desires that can be preyed upon. There is endless demand for the snake oil that purports to reveal the secrets to vast wealth. This demand for books, DVDs, and seminars comes from the human bias toward the exciting versus the mundane. Our focus needs to be on the mundane. The true road to financial strength lies in ownership, discipline, and long-term patience. The goal must be to master the discipline and fundamentals of consistent rational decision making over the course of our entire lives.

The vast majority of us are never going to break through to the dream of vast wealth. This is simple realism. The important work of nursing, teaching, policing, plumbing, and all the things that provide livelihood for the majority of the population is never going to create great windfalls of money. That does not mean that hardworking American investors will not be able to create strength through discipline and rational long-term investing. The goal should be to optimize our own potential, not dream of grandiosity that is unlikely to ever be achieved.

The dreams of immense wealth and riches cause neglect of the very essential things that can actually be done to create relative strength and prosperity. We all have that germ of the idea that there will somehow be a pot of gold at the end of the proverbial rainbow. We should also know that there will be no gold and maybe not even a pot to put our pennies in! What all this big thinking does is blot out all the small steps that we must take from the earliest possible point in our working lives.

Focusing on the grandiose instead of the practical is a horrible defect of American culture. It seems obvious that most hardworking individuals will never become rich. Yet, we continue to witness more and more of these kinds of dreams being sold. The stock trading systems, no money down real estate deals, and how-to guides have been around for years, but things have been getting worse; I recently saw a system for trading currency futures! You might as well buy a system for playing casino slot machines.

This brings us to an old mathematical truth that I would like to retread for this discussion. The compounding of money over time is the most important thing we can learn or teach. The chart below illustrates the dramatic difference in the results of those who begin saving early.

The assumptions are that both parties save $2,400 per year ($200 per month). The money each saves earns 7 percent growth per year.

This chart has been recycled frequently in many different financial books. It should be helpful in understanding that building financial strength is a lot like a race in which we compete with ourselves. The key is to begin running the race. The sooner we get out the $6.60 per day that almost anyone can afford, the greater the result will be. The leverage of time is what must be understood and recognized as the most powerful element that can be harnessed.

Contribution Per Month	$200		
7% Average Annual Return	Start Now	Wait 10 Years	Difference
Portfolio Value after 5 years	$ 14,285	$ -	$ 14,285
Portfolio Value after 10 years	$ 34,320	$ -	$ 34,320
Portfolio Value after 15 years	$ 62,420	$ 14,285	$ 48,136
Portfolio Value after 20 years	$ 101,833	$ 34,320	$ 67,513

The ultimate numbers in the chart are not what is important; rather, it is the difference in value for those who have the good fortune to begin early. Note that the 7 percent return is purely hypothetical, and our investment would never grow at this rate as depicted in the chart. To achieve a 7 percent return, there would be many down years along the way, without any certainty of ever achieving 10 percent returns.

Many people will go through life in a state of financial weakness and irresponsibility with the conscious or subconscious notion that one day they will get started on "a plan." Others will dream of somehow making a "big score" and ending up secure. The vast majority of the population simply lives month to month, without ever acknowledging that no winning lottery ticket is going to bail them out. The greatest single example of this jackpot mindset is the proliferation lottery games. It is tragic to see the popularity of all these silly gambling opportunities located in every gas station, liquor store, and pharmacy chain. I proudly maintain that I have never purchased a single lottery ticket. I admit that I have had dreams of how I would handle the vast fortune that I see people win, but I have always seen that the odds of winning are less than that of being struck by lightning.

A large number of people buy these tickets to a dream every month. But, has anyone ever sat down and looked at the mathematical probability of winning? The lottery is just another tax that the government has instituted to draw money from a mathematically unaware populace. In the aggregate, all the money that goes into the multitude of ever expanding lotteries would make a huge difference if it were invested by people instead of cycled through government spending. I have seen estimates that as much as $40 billion per year is "wagered" on various lotteries. The slogan should be, "Lottery … the ultimate symbol of financial ignorance and denial."

In my daily practice, I see this dynamic in many ways. Living beyond our means is another sad by-product of the big dream mentality. Expensive vacations are a great example where people use up cash for a few fleeting days of fun in the sun. I don't want to sound like a killjoy, but it seems that nowadays people expect travel and extravagance year after year.

Elaborate vacations, cruises, Disneyland, and the like seem to be some sort of rite of passage. The travel "industry" has spawned from our consumption culture. Previous generations took a road trip or maybe one or two significant vacations during the years when the family could all travel and enjoy the time together. Down the road, all of that money that could have been harnessed into portfolio building and retirement saving is reduced to some pictures and memories. What is so important to understand is that once we begin to have a strong portfolio, it can begin to help pay for our vacations.

I believe the modern American assumes that one will work a career and then somehow end up with a sunny Florida retirement. The era of 1965 to 1995 is not going to be replicated. People have been greatly influenced by the generations of people who had guaranteed pensions and health insurance. That is a deceptively generous era of financial history. Going forward, those who do not create their own pension plan, including health care dollars, are deluding themselves. We are now in an era where the 401(k) is the core retirement asset. For those who do not manage it correctly, there will be no money at all, let alone some endless vacation in a warm sunny climate.

The generations before the baby boomers were not jetsetters. The history books are filled with stories of sacrifice and diligent saving. Often, we see references to the "Depression-era" mindset. I think that type of cautious thinking can be useful. Saving and investing until it hurts throughout one's working life will never be looked back on as a mistake. I am not advocating that we live and work only to save and invest every penny; but rather that we focus on the power of consistent saving and rational investing decisions.

Once you incorporate a consistent practice of rational investing techniques, you can add more and more luxury to your life. The key is to consistently save and invest throughout one's working career. All too often, I see people go many years before saving anything. The key point to understand and believe is that once the portfolio gains greater and greater value, you can begin to add more and more to the disposable budget.

Once again, our culture is reflecting the idea of, "I want it big and I want it now." Nassim Nicholas Taleb writes of a concept of "extremistan" in his intriguing work, *The Black Swan*. Taleb implores us to see that the modern world has evolved into a place where events are difficult to predict and can be quite extreme in their impact. I think this concept applies very well to the current landscape of American culture when it comes to the idea of emulating the "billionaire next door" or "rich mom, poor daughter" or any of the other silly titles that I see perpetually sold to people seeking a formula for their financial security.

There is no secret formula or recipe. It all comes back to the opposite of the extreme: A balanced financial diet weighted toward ownership. Discipline, patience, and a long-term vision for the maximization of every individual's potential is the goal.

Nothing New Under the Sun

"There's only one corner of the universe you can be certain of improving, and that's your own self."

Aldous Huxley

With a high degree of cynicism, Ron Shink said to me on many occasions, "Dave, there's nothing new under the sun." This did not make sense to me for a long time. Eventually, I came to define this to myself as an expression of the fact that most ideas that sound like something new are recycled from previous things, but with a new wrapper. If you want to be deep and philosophical, you can think in terms of everything that the earth has in and on it has been here from the beginning.

At this point, I am sure you are aware that I am highly skeptical of new ideas. There are certainly ongoing improvements being made every day. There certainly are great financial products that are huge improvements from 20 or even 10 years ago. The main caveat is that the ideas that look great today were a small group of survivors from the plethora of things that were introduced. It is important to form a perspective that includes all the bad ideas that did not survive. The hot programs of today will only reveal flaws over time.

On a recent trip to a local drug store, I was struck by the sheer quantity of choices of soaps and lotions. It is simply incredible to contemplate the variations of aloe vera, avocado, and green tea that can be incorporated into these products. I estimate that three or four types would cover most of the requirements of the human race. However, the companies that produce soaps and lotions continue to refine their products for the enhancement of profits, not necessarily for the goal of greater human hygiene. Financial companies do essentially the same thing, but it can be much more damaging to the consumer.

Recently, I grabbed this ad from a national newspaper: "Introducing the retirement funds you don't have to rebalance, reallocate, revise or re-anything … just choose a retirement date as far out as 10, 20 or even 30 years." The terminology for this is "target date" funds. This is a new concept that is being heavily sold to the public. "Wow, I can simply turn my retirement over to this new system and forget about it." This was from a discount brokerage company that markets products directly to the public.

How very ironic that a financial firm that caters to those who want to "do it themselves" has come up with this. "Gee, it's just like a guaranteed pension." That is what people want. They want to just turn over their money, and call up in 30 years and start receiving their monthly checks!

The sad part is that billions of dollars will flow into another new, untested financial idea. The assumption is that the formula of future financial security has been discovered. If it has, it really eliminates the need for many financial institutions, and certainly advisors are unnecessary. There is a huge wave of these types of targeted investment products now coming on the scene. I am very skeptical of what the results will be.

Targeted investment products are examples of a newly marketed financial product. They usually revolve around the concept of an asset allocation mutual fund that gradually becomes more conservative as time goes by and the target date draws closer. The target date can be 10, 20, or more years from the purchase date. We can place our investment and know that it will be very low in risk by the time that the target date arrives.

The concept of a target date mutual fund is new and untested. In the last five years, I have seen numerous revisions to many of the products that have been sold to consumers. Revisions and changes to the programs are an obvious sign of defect in the underlying concept. The changes have often involved the amount of equities to include in a given allocation. This is the critical element that could end up costing a large amount in lost growth.

A larger problem is that we are making the difficult job of managing money even more complex. A fund targeted 20 years from now will start out as a growth fund and then gradually morph into a balanced and ultimately an income fund. Growth investing is much different than balanced or income investing. How will the fund modify its management culture as changing tactics and new strategies will become necessary?

The truly troubling part for me is that these types of targeted products are being promoted with the implication that they are proven. There is absolutely no proof that this will be beneficial to the small investor or 401(k) participant. These concepts are being driven by the idea that things are just too darn complex for the little guy and the big, friendly, objective mutual fund company will take care of everything.

The sheer volume of new financial products that I have seen introduced is overwhelming. Financial product companies, including mutual fund groups and insurance companies, are constantly looking to distinguish themselves through the creation of new financial products. Most of the products introduced are not even close to worthy of an investor's precious college fund or retirement money.

Annuities are another example of a product that is constantly re-engineered by insurance companies. As a financial advisor, I am bombarded every year with solicitations to sell to my clients the latest and greatest annuity. Rarely do I see last year's great program or a great annuity from five years ago. Endless revisions, name changes, new money managers, and other changes make it very difficult to compare 10-year track records.

New and improved is often an effort to eliminate that tough sell of poor previous performance. One of the benefits of limiting the search for quality money management to the 200 largest mutual funds is that we will rarely find the latest fad or a newly engineered fund that has not been tested. Often I will see small start-up funds post huge results over one or even three years. The fund will then begin to attract money quickly and the early high returns will often prove to be difficult to replicate. For the shareholder, these small funds become difficult to own with confidence when they become volatile.

I believe it is of paramount importance that a given money manager, mutual fund, or other vehicle have at least a 10-year track record of quality results before one invests in that fund. It is difficult for any money manager or mutual fund company to start a fund today, place in a realistic amount of seed capital, and wait 10 years. This is not a very good business proposition! This is why it is important to most financial product companies to create some kind of new technique or breakthrough to attract your money. If it doesn't work out, the fund can always be merged, the manager can be fired, and the company can start over. Glitz, marketing, and compelling stories are much easier to dream up than the slow difficult process of patient, quality money management.

Starting over is a big part of what's "new" in money management. In recent research that I conducted, I found many money management companies that offer asset allocation services to advisors and the public had introduced many new programs and services in 2001 and 2002. Gee, what was happening in that time frame … oh yes, that was the bottom of one of the worst bear markets of the last 30 years! Many money managers simply began anew. Check it out. Look for 10-year track records. Many do exist and look pretty bad. There are many others out there with inception dates in 2001 and 2002. That was a great time to get a fresh start and to shed the horrible performance that many funds had produced.

Many of these companies have all sorts of stories to tell about the new programs and how they are going to produce returns in the future. I usually tell their sales reps to call me when they have a 10-year track record that reflects quality. I do not get too many return calls.

As of this writing, the most powerful example of financial product innovation gone sour is the securitization of mortgage contracts. The concept that allowed your local bank to sell your mortgage to a Wall Street investment bank instead of being the lender has blown up completely. Lately, the biggest financial firms in the world are very busy disclosing massive losses projected to be as much as $500 billion or more.

The endless advertising of mortgage companies proclaiming "no cost" and "no money down" services turned out to have a lot of hidden, bundled, and built-in costs. The stream of advertising messages was a great indicator of the bad things to come. It is another strong example that things that are marketed very heavily are usually dangerous to the consumer and should be avoided.

The story this year is often referred to as "the sub-prime mortgage crisis." I have been particularly angry at the way the lending industry has become such a heavy marketer of complex and dangerous financial products. I have felt strongly for quite some time that consumers have been misled and preyed upon by lightly regulated marketers selling loans like the latest designer fashion. In my 43 short years on this earth, I can remember a time when there were no television advertisements for mortgages. Until the recent wave of massive losses, these types of ads were some of the most frequent of any that I have witnessed. Just another novel financial product structure that didn't work out! These products may prove to have triggered the greatest systemic financial crisis in the history of the United States.

The consequences of commission-driven mortgage products are now being exposed. This is a dramatic example of a financial product that was driven by sales commissions geared to higher compensation for the sales rep when he or she could get you to take more risk or assume higher costs. These lenders who sold people on pulling equity out of their homes with deceptive adjustable-rate loans will simply regroup and dream up a new structure that can be manufactured and sold to some other group of vulnerable, ill-informed consumers. The sense is that if you had your home repossessed or were forced into bankruptcy, it must be your own fault.

One may wonder what might have happened if all mortgage broker commissions had been disclosed in a simple and understandable way. A better environment might have been experienced if the products were compensation neutral—meaning the sales rep would not have been motivated to recommend the interest-only, pay-what-you-want adjustable mortgage garbage that was sold to people. Much of this pain could have been avoided if consumers could have sought the counsel of objective, fee-compensated debt advisors who could have helped compare financing strategies. This is another in a never-ending stream of examples of what the financial services complex produces when the distribution system is based on a loosely regulated, commission-based compensation system.

The mortgage crisis of 2007 to 2008 is a stark illustration of what happens when "new" financial products are invented and marketed to the undereducated mass market consumer. How could the average person understand the consequences of "interest only" or "one-year adjustable" mortgages in an environment of economic and real estate slowdown? The answer is found in the reality that these products were created not through natural demand of the marketplace, but rather through the complex mortgage products synthesized deep in the catacombs of Wall Street.

Structured pools of mortgages were an invention of the 1970s. For many years prior to that, banks held loans in their own portfolio until they matured or were paid off. In February 1970, the US Department of Housing and Urban Development conducted a transaction using a mortgage-backed security. Securitization of debt allowed for great expansion of lending as the vast suburbs and exurbs were built in the United States over the next 35 years. A massive amount of capital became available not only for housing, but securitization was adapted to auto loans, credit card debt, and virtually all forms of borrowing.

As these mortgage pools evolved to become increasingly complex, unintended consequences were (of course) unleashed. The relationship between the bank and the homeowner essentially no longer existed. The local bank now was simply a sales office for loans that would be resold into pools of mortgages packaged by the biggest names of American finance. A massive and hugely profitable mortgage loan industry was nurtured and exploited by behemoths like Citigroup, Merrill Lynch, and AIG, to name a few. Most borrowers would never understand that when sitting in the bank, they were actually in the den of commission-driven money sales reps. Money was being packaged and sold to consumer borrowers as a product, with little regulation and minimal disclosure.

The bankers, who had traditionally underwritten the risk of each loan, were no longer subject to such restraints. The retail banks were only interested in selling money. The marketing was comical to watch. "Bad credit? No problem!" "No documentation of your income? We can get you a loan real quick!" The advertising was relentless. The only goal was closing deals. People with bad credit history become the most desirable because they paid the highest fees and interest rates. The lending industry even had a nice professional-sounding name for its sales-people ... loan officers!

The fallout from this mortgage debacle will impact our economy for many years. The human suffering caused by so many being encouraged to borrow with no regard for the long-term dream of home equity is the saddest aspect of this damage, but that are many other areas of pain. Builders, tradesmen, and customer service workers are just a few of the professions that will be affected for years.

The lending industry will recover, as will many of the professions that rely on lending and housing. The United States will remain a highly desirable place to own property. My hope as I watch our Federal Reserve frantically cut interest rates and the US Congress send out tax "rebate" checks is that a more responsible system of lending may emerge. One of the core problems under this current structure that was driven by securitization is that the actual borrower and lender were many steps removed from each other. This separation generated huge fees for the securitizers and processors of these loans and pools of loans.

The huge fees that the investment banks were able to generate will not be forgotten as new laws are crafted to resolve the problems that transpired. As long as a lender has no fiduciary responsibility to the borrowing party in a transaction, I fear that we will see other episodes like this in the lending industry's future. The lobbying will be mammoth, from the large Wall Street firms to the banks and non-bank lenders, there will eventually be industry-crafted legislation created to "fix" this problem. The real fix is for borrowers and consumers of all type to be keenly aware that the lenders are operating strictly in the interests of their own institution's profitability.

The lesson that we need to draw from junk bond debacles, tech-stock manias, and mortgage crises is the same: healthy skepticism. Beware the highly processed, synthesized products that give you the quick boost today. Only old, established, proven, and boring mutual funds, 30- or 15-year fixed mortgages, and the hard work of saving, borrowing, and investing that have proven themselves over long periods of time are healthy for your financial body.

Many of today's financial products have grown increasingly synthetic. Just like synthesized food (think of the wonderful invention of Olestra, the synthetic fat), there are all kinds of new problems created by the alchemy. As I have emphasized repeatedly throughout this work, the more complex and opaque something becomes, the more reason to avoid it.

Investment Zen

"Everyone should carefully observe which way his heart draws him, and then choose that way with all his strength."

Hasidic Saying

Investing success is very similar to other forms of accomplishment and happiness in life. It is not determined by how much or how fast we may accumulate (although making a lot of dough quick would always be nice), but rather our commitment to the process. The path to financial strength is a difficult one filled with panics, manias, false promises, and endless stressful events along the way.

There is an old investing proverb that advises to "buy when blood is flowing in the streets." It sounds obvious that when prices are low you should accumulate. The actual experience of severe down markets is quite another story. We are witnessing these very dynamics now with stock market and housing prices in the United States and around the developed world. People do not want to buy and then watch prices decline further; thus, a vicious circle is formed and prices will overshoot on the downside. The natural human desire to get the best value will cause many to wait too long or never act to take advantage of the bargains that are being created. These down times are the most difficult tests for investors.

Markets are known to overshoot on both the upside and the downside. When the average investor comes to the market with new money, the allure of what is working now is very powerful. The current landscape of commodity mania is a good example. The story is so compelling that it is very difficult to resist the higher and higher prices posted every day. Every expert I see is talking about the importance of commodities in the allocation of a well-diversified portfolio.

We, of course, also have to face the doom and gloom of the "experts" who talk of using up the world's resources. This has been a recurring theme since the use of whale blubber as fuel. The notion that humans will exhaust the Earth's resources ignores the power of human innovation. In a time where the emerging economies of China and India are industrializing at an incredible pace, these theories become quite compelling. The doom and gloom that continually arises must roll down our investment back without a second thought.

The vision of these emerging market countries as similar to the United States in their patterns of consumption and production is similar to the fears of Japan in the 1980s. As energy prices rise, the comparative advantage of cheap labor or lax environmental protections becomes less of an advantage and global economic competition will likely cool the rate of growth in the developing world. America is the leader of the world in innovation and wealth creation, and it is a place that many look to come to work and live. Betting against the United States has never been a good proposition.

The end of the petroleum age will most likely come from innovation, not from lack of supply. The higher prices of commodities are accelerating the incentives for innovation. The investments in cleaner, renewable fuel sources that did not make economic sense at $30-a-barrel oil now are being rabidly pursued. The opportunity facing the free world will likely look incredible in 5 to 15 years as we see massive parts of the transportation infrastructure proceed through an upgrade cycle. All of the inefficient trucks and oil-based manufacturing processes are subject to replacement. Those that fear global recession due to a commodity price spiral ignore these facts of economics and human ingenuity. I eagerly wait for the day that the US Post Office declares that it will invest in renewable fuel or natural gas delivery trucks! That will be a small but powerful sign that the game is on.

These innovation forces are difficult to see during a crisis. "This too shall pass" is such an important cliché to remind ourselves as investors. The innovations of the future will present great investment returns to those who accumulate quality. No one can predict where the great global economic engines will come from. Do not look for accurate forecasts; they will likely be way off the mark. No one predicted the change of advertising to the Internet and search engine technology. No prediction engine will ever be developed to help our human brains overcome the uncertainty that is the future. This future uncertainty is the dilemma that creates opportunity for investors, not the fear mongering of the predictors of doom who have always been proven wrong.

What we can control as investors is our attitude and patience for the process. As we have discussed throughout these chapters, one of the key lessons to success is to learn to own quality investments regardless of the current market valuation that may reflect this year's price. Raw technology, manufacturing innovation, agriculture production refinements, and transportation solutions are some the areas that we need to seek as long-term investors, not coal or gold or oil. Trying to own commodities at the right time is a form of market timing.

The personality traits of successful investors are the very same traits that make for success in many areas of life:

1. Investors do not give up.

During bad times, experienced, long-term investors do not panic or make big changes. They look to past crises and the rewarding recoveries that followed and hold their quality investments. Successful investors continue to buy if they are in the accumulation phase of life and feel lucky to be able to buy at reduced prices.

2. Understand what you own.

The key to success is in the understanding of what investing really is. Knowing what you own will prove invaluable when the down markets come. So many who panic will look and conclude, "My 401(k) lost $XX and I need to sell now!" What if that same person had inherited the corner gas station? Would he rush to sell it during a bad economy? When we understand our investments as the ownership that they are, with all the risk and rewards that the owners reap, we will be much more likely to act with understanding and prudence.

This market timing mentality is what will cause the most stress and anxiety to the investor's psyche. That is why the lessons of Zen and emotional balance can be so very central to our profile of the ideal investor.

"A gem is not polished without rubbing, nor a man perfected without trials." Chinese Proverb

"Should you desire the great tranquility, prepare to sweat white beads." Zen Master Hakuin

Detachment from our current situation is a key ingredient in the pursuit of fulfillment. In our process for investing, it is critical to release our focus on a particular gain or loss in market value. The process of life and the happiness that we all seek is long and difficult. It is different for all of us, and so it is with our investments. Often I am asked, "How much do I need to retire or be secure?" The answer is different for everyone. Do you want to live in a northern Michigan rural community with lower costs of living? Some will want a Chicago condo and a winter home in Arizona. The goal will be very different, depending on many factors and lifestyle choices.

No number will lead to a perfect outcome. The rewards are in the process. The process of creating a strong secure financial foundation, for our lives and our legacy, is what great inspiration can be made of. The difficult but attainable goal of patience, discipline, and understanding as the owner/investor takes time and risk for the rewards of strength and security. I think it is one of the most worthy pursuits that one can hope to achieve.

Our American culture has grown "over the top." We have become a people of "over-the-topism." From triple beef bacon cheeseburgers to nine-passenger, all-terrain vehicles, our consumption ethos has usurped the American ethic of sacrifice and sweat that helps each successive generation live at a higher standard of living. Instant credit and no-money-down financing have created a culture that seeks consumption above all else. American lives and decisions need to be based on an understanding of the ever present complex forces that shape our world. We need to be better consumers by discriminating against the pointless products that are continuously marketed down our collective throats.

As we become more selective in our everyday choices, the investment decisions and amount we can save will likely be enhanced. Our investments will then be more likely to "grow up" and live into their fifteenth year and beyond. As that long-term discipline and consistency shows itself in ownership wealth, we can begin to live the dream of security and control of our destiny. At that point, the joy of grandchildren and helping sow the seeds of success in our precious descendents can then come into focus.

Ownership is the key to financial success. The dream of your own business is not a fantasy. It can be the product of years of patient, disciplined saving and investing. A well-diversified, quality portfolio *is* the dream of ownership. The worthy goal of owning your own business is attainable to all investors, large and small. This reality of ownership can help shape a better world as we Americans become better consumers, investors, and exemplar citizens of this Earth. We can live our lives as a beacon to the rest of the world, with democratic capitalism, ownership, and responsible consumption creating a better future that is America.

Definitions and Terms

After-Tax Return   The net return of a given investment after taxes have been paid.

Bear Market   A market downturn that is 20 percent or more over a prolonged period.

Blue Chip   Stock of a well-established company that usually pays regular dividends and carries no extensive liabilities.

Bull Market   Period of rising investor confidence with rising general stock prices and market indexes.

CD   Certificate of deposit. Savings deposit made for a fixed term, usually available for terms ranging from three months to five years.

Debt   Created when a creditor or lender agrees to lend money or assets to a debtor. There are many variations, including private debt, public debt, secured and unsecured debt.

Diversification   Mixing of a wide variety of investments with the aim of reducing risk.

Dividend   Payment made by a corporation to stockholders. Can be changed (increased or suspended) at the discretion of the corporate board.

Dollar Cost Averaging   Investing a level or gradually increasing amount on a periodic basis; may reduce risk of making a single large purchase.

Economist   Expert in social science theory that may involve statistics, econometrics, and philosophical theories in efforts to model markets, behavior, and various types of financial phenomena.

Equity Broad concept of share of ownership, the amount of value one has; non-debt securities.

Exchange-Traded Fund (ETF) Stock-like investment vehicle, traded on stock exchanges. Most track an index; can be low cost, and provide tax efficiency.

Fiduciary One who has a legal bond to act for and on behalf of another whose funds are entrusted to the fiduciary for investment; the highest standard of care. A fiduciary is expected to be extremely loyal to the principal (beneficiary).

FIC Financial-Industrial Complex The concept of a group of forces that include insurance, investment, and other types of financial firms creating an environment (through lobbying the government) that maximizes profits to the industry as the primary or only goal at the expense of the consumer/investor.

Forecast Attempt to predict the future; usually done by smart-sounding people who have no established record for their past forecasts.

Hedge Fund Manager of a pool of funds that is less regulated than mainstream mutual funds. Open only to a limited range of investors (accredited investors) and may take on leverage, short sales, or conduct other high-risk activities that regulated mutual funds cannot.

Index Method of measuring the general stock market or sector of the stock market through the tracking of a specified group of stocks. Many indexes have become investments products available to individual investors.

Inflation Rise in the general level of prices for goods or services that has generally occurred in a given economy over time; decline in purchasing power or "real" value of money.

Inflation Risk The loss in value of money that may be held in low-growth savings or investment vehicles over time.

IRA Individual retirement account. A retirement plan account that provides tax advantages; usually contains income that has not yet been taxed.

Loanership The practice of making long-term investments in debt and interest-bearing instruments.

Proprietary Product Financial product (mutual fund, annuity) that is sold and serviced by employees of the creator of the product; often can only be held by the financial company that created it.

Prospectus Legal document filed with the Securities and Exchange Commission that mutual funds (or other institutions) use to delineate and describe the securities that are offered for purchase.

Real Interest Rate The rate of growth of a given account or investment after deducting the effect of inflation.

Registered Investment Advisor A person or firm that has registered with the Securities and Exchange Commission or a state regulatory agency; a designation that does not denote any necessary formal training beyond an FINRA series 65 exam, but rather an indication that the individual or firm is so registered and subjected itself to the requirements of the regulator; considered to be acting as a fiduciary.

Registered Representative An individual who is licensed to sell securities; legal power of an agent, required to pass FINRA series 7 and 63 exams (or series 6 exam for limited securities activity).

Roth IRA Individual retirement account created by Taxpayer Relief Act of 1997. Contains non-deductible contributions that may be tax free if held to age 59½.

Simple IRA Employer-provided salary reduction plan with low complexity and employer liability.

Small Cap A firm with a market capitalization below a certain threshold, usually between $10 or $20 billion, generally more volatile and risky for investors.

Tax Deferred To delay paying taxes to a future time, generally used in reference to tax-deductible investments such as 401(k), 403(b), and various types of IRAs.

Top 200 Fund   Mutual fund that ranks in the upper 200 based on amount of assets under management.

Total Return   The measurement of a given investment return, including any dividends and capital gains paid to the owner.

Track Record   The history of performance of a given investment, often stated in 1-, 3-, 5-, 10-year increments; provides no guarantee of future results.

Value Averaging   Technique that attempts to invest an amount that will increase the investment by a target increment. May produce higher results than basic dollar cost averaging.

Volatility   Another term for the statistical measurement of standard deviation; often used as an indication of the risk of an investment over a given historical time period.

Yield   The nonprice-related returns of an investment; that is, a bond may have a 4 percent coupon yield, but may return more or less if sold before maturity.

Printed in the United States
135490LV00002B/2/P